AUERBACH ON
COMPUTER OUTPUT
MICROFILM

AUERBACH ON series

Published:

Optical Character Recognition
Alphanumeric Displays
Automatic Photocomposition
Microfilm Readers/Printers
Digital Plotters and Image Digitizers
Computer Output Microfilm

Coming:

Data Collection Systems
Data Communications Terminals
Small Business Computers
Software for Business Accounting
Time Sharing
Data Entry Systems
Minicomputers
Data Communications
Systems Software
Large Scale Memories

AUERBACH ON

COMPUTER OUTPUT
MICROFILM

AUERBACH®
publishers

princeton
philadelphia
new york
london

Library of Congress Catalog Card Number: 70-171052
International Standard Book Number: 0-87769-105-3

First Printing

Printed in the United States of America

CONTENTS

PREFACE

This volume is one of a series of books covering significant developments in the information science industry. *AUERBACH On Computer Output Microfilm* is written for those who need only to familiarize themselves with COM technology rather than master it. Owing to the way its various subjects are separated, as much or as little of the discussion can be read in accordance with actual need. This volume can therefore serve as a reference as readily as a primary information source.

Sad to say, the story of computer output microfilm so far is in many ways like a tale of unrequited love. Those who have nurtured it with both mind and materiel, and even many believers who eventually joined the mystique with the commitment of actual installation, have met disappointment. The marketers of COM have been consistently denied the profits that a succession of surveys over many years has foretold; the operators of surprisingly many installations, furthermore, are still waiting for promised savings and greater operating efficiency. In short, the love of the aficionados has not yet been requited with the monetary rewards that were prophesied.

In conceding what is nothing more than an indisputable fact, we do not mean to distort the truth or to exaggerate it. Although little if any profit has been realized so far by the manufacturers, there are innumerable COM installations that have achieved their goals and are contributing invaluable benefits to their operators. Meanwhile, announcements of new COM equipment are made periodically, and faith in the concept will not die. Sales continue to advance at a steady pace, if not a spectacular one. Obviously, there must be much intrinsic merit in the idea.

This volume of the AUERBACH ON series affords an opportunity to look at computer output microfilm afresh. It examines the history of its development and expounds its unquestionably exciting concepts and potentialities. These impressions are enlarged by a thorough discussion of all aspects of technology, including a glimpse into future design trends. Much information is furnished on specific products and their manufacturers, part of which consists of comparison chart summaries in Appendix I. In short, the anatomy of COM is dissected and put back together without any beating of drums.

There is a reason for this disinterested approach, aside from the obvious need for fairness: COM can be extremely advantageous in some environments and less than useful in others. This book should provide the careful reader with the required insight to evaluate his own situation and determine the suitability of COM for his requirements.

AUERBACH On Computer Output Microfilm is an expansion of material derived from *AUERBACH Graphic Processing Reports.* This publication is a major unit in the *AUERBACH Computer Technology Reports,* a loose-leaf reference service recognized as the standard guide to EDP throughout the world. It is prepared and edited by the publisher's staff of professional EDP specialists.

Material in this volume was prepared by the staff of AUERBACH Publishers Inc., and has been updated prior to publication. Nevertheless, any book on a dynamic technological subject is foredoomed to be at least a little out of date even when it first appears. Strict currentness and completeness of this volume therefore cannot be guaranteed. Information can be obtained from AUERBACH Publishers Inc., 121 North Broad Street, Philadelphia, Pa. 19107.

1. THE RISE OF A NEW CONCEPT

For each new need that confronts him, man eventually finds a way to fashion a new tool that serves his purpose. The digital computer, devised originally to perform rapid calculations and later adapted to innumerable other functions as well, has by its very success created the need for commensurate speed on the part of output devices connected to it.

Even in its infancy the computer was churning data at a rate approaching 100,000 characters per second. Certainly an impact printer, struggling during that period in the 1950s to maintain 1500 characters per second, did not belong in the same race. Even more critical was the problem of outputting graphic data. Some attempts were made to interface analog plotters to computers, and soon afterward the automatic digital plotter was introduced, but the outcome in both cases was dismal. Even if these early plotters had not compounded the problem with unreliability, their sluggish operation was hopeless compared with the speed of the computer. Altogether, the only effective output device was the cathode-ray tube (CRT).

Although the cathode-ray tube responds instantaneously to applied signals, the information vanishes forever once its display screen is erased. Photographing oscilloscope patterns with a Polaroid camera was already an established engineering practice in the 1950s. Many computer practitioners must have independently followed this engineering precedent by hanging a camera in front of their cathode-ray tube display. This first merging of the three high-speed technologies—the computer, the cathode-

1

ray tube display, and photography—marked the dawn of computer output microfilming, or COM.

DEFINITION OF COM

Two further steps are required, however, to create a true computer output microfilmer. One is the introduction of a camera that records on microfilm or microfiche. The other is the development of coordinated processes that not only convert the coded information generated by the computer into the various signals required at the cathode-ray tube, but also effectuate the precise registering of the displayed image onto the specified film position and automatically advance either the film or the camera to the next frame position.

With the advent of the Memorex 1603 microfilm printer early in 1970, a new imaging technique has appeared. The light-emitting ability of certain semiconductors, called light-emitting diodes, or LED, is utilized to form characters by illuminating specified diodes in an array in accordance with the familiar dot-matrix principle. After each line of characters is printed, it is recorded and the film is then advanced to the next position. In cathode-ray tube imaging, the entire frame is completed before the film is incremented.

Today a computer output microfilmer is defined as a system of hardware components that converts digitized computer output into a corresponding image of alphanumerics or graphic forms and automatically records successive images on a precisely registered and sequenced microformat. It should be noted that the ability to record graphic forms as well as alphanumeric gives COMS an important advantage over impact printers.

HISTORY

In the late 1950s and early 1960s, prototypes of today's COM devices were built by Stromberg-DatagraphiX, California Computer Products, Computer Industries (now the University Computing Company), Eastman Kodak, IBM, and Data Display, Inc. of St. Paul. Kodak's development during the 1950s was known as DACOM. The IBM 2280 and the dd80 (currently known as the CDC 280) were CRT printer-plotters capable of plotting up to 220,000 points per second. They were designed particularly for military, engineering, and scientific markets. Some machines were sold, but since the future looked dubious, the devices were shelved. In particular, IBM departed from the field categorically. Kodak returned in 1969 with

KOM-90, based in part on its original work, and recently announced the lower-priced KOM-80. Control Data has utilized its Data Display subsidiary primarily to develop graphic display terminals. The IBM 4481 film reader/recorder announced in May 1970 demonstrates IBM's renewed interest in microfilm and in digitized film images, but not necessarily in COM.

Without question, the true pioneer of the industry was Stromberg-DatagraphiX, but the activity of California Computer Products should not be overlooked. In 1958 DatagraphiX brought out a special model for the Social Security Administration and followed it in 1960 with the SC-4020. The company also took the decisive step of assigning salesmen to its promotion. These early efforts produced only a limited number of sales. Today, with such additional COM products as the 4060, 4360, and 4440, DatagraphiX enjoys a larger population of installations than any other company. However, since DatagraphiX was virtually alone in the industry until 1968, its present market share of less than 50 percent represents not a gain but a fall from dominance. CalComp, meanwhile, has adhered to its tradition of concentrating on printer-plotters.

Possibly the most widely accepted COM system so far has been the Memorex 1603 microfilm printer. To counter this competition from Memorex and other companies, whose recorders offer advanced features and the latest design technology, DatagraphiX announced in September 1970 the 4200 Micromation on-line microfilmer (MOM). This late surge by the industry leader to be competitive suggests that a new era for COM is now unfolding. Earlier in the year, CalComp had countered with the 1670 microfilm printer-plotter.

Supporting the view of a new era is the wide gulf that separates recent models from their ancestors of the early 1960s. In the beginning, COM was simply a marriage of convenience between existing graphic terminals and photo-optical systems that had been developed during World War II. Today there is renewed interest in photo-optical techniques, of which the universal cameras developed by Vought and Stromberg-DatagraphiX are but one example. Another is the new imaging techniques that have been perfected. One is the previously mentioned LED method in conjunction with fiber-optic light conductors, and another is electron-beam recording developed by the 3M Company. These developments will be explained later.

OTHER REASONS FOR COM

Basically, the attractiveness of COM can be epitomized by saying that it offers a promise of significant cost savings. Although the potential for savings definitely exists, later discussion in this report will show that for the unwary purchaser the promise can easily be unfulfilled. The COM cost equation, of course, has many implicit factors. For example, the packing density of data imprinted on a microformat is extremely high—about a million and a half data bits per linear inch for reduction ratios in the order of 20X. Film as a consumable supply is inherently cheap. It is light in weight, and microfilm or microfiche by its nature is compressed in size. For example, a 100-foot roll of film weighs less than a pound, including the cassette, and rests comfortably in the hand. The same statement can hardly be made about a stack of computer printout paper comprising a like number of images, even when the roll holds only 2000 or 2400 frames. With respect to volume, the cassette occupies less than 1 percent as much space as the paper stack.

Consultation of a postal rate schedule would disclose how much more costly than film is the distribution of paper. Both microfilm and microfiche are much more amenable to storage and retrieval coding and subsequent automatic search techniques than is paper. Thus, microfilm not only saves storage space, but also can be retrieved in about one-ninth the time of recapturing paper. Not more than six copies can be conveniently printed by an impact printer, but an unlimited number of duplicates can be made from a master film. Under conditions of quality production, this cost can be less than 1/10 cent a page.

The preceding discussion can be summarized by remarking that the development of COM was also spurred by the desire to escape from the bulk, expense, and general nuisance of handling paper. As the progressive minority utilizing microfilm today knows so well, paper is heavy and unwieldy; it is expensive to store and distribute, relatively expensive to print, relatively difficult to retrieve, and expensive to duplicate in large quantities.

A collateral benefit of dispensing with paper is the elimination of decollating, bursting, and binding information. This gain, of course, augments other incentives to generate ever greater volumes of document pages. From this standpoint it might be argued that computer output microfilm intensifies the problem of retrieval, but the medium, as we have already seen, is ideally suited for this purpose.

If the mechanical liabilities of impact printers are considered disadvantageous, the substitution of a COM recorder will be beneficial as long as it is more reliable than the machine replaced. The virtue of many older microfilmers, unfortunately, is doubted by disillusioned users. Caution is therefore needed in appraising the newer designs that employ semiconductor electronics and advanced photo-optical systems with high-response, digitally pulsed servos. Yet, even as performance data is being evaluated, this new breed of microfilmer gives signs of attaining a substantially up-graded operational integrity.

User surveys show that once operators make the transition to micro-film and its accessories, they often feel that the displayed image offers clearer print than paper printouts and that using film and viewers (readers) is physically more comfortable than working from paper. Whether this view is a majority or minority attitude can be argued, but it is interesting nonetheless.

DISADVANTAGES OF COM

The most critical disadvantage of microfilm systems—COM systems included—is the human factors problem associated with them. The un-familiarity of film to many people creates resistance to a microfilm system. This basic aversion is accentuated by user inexperience with reading and searching film, the lack of hard copy when a printer is not available, and the limited access of microfilm readers. These interrelated factors may induce those who contemplate automating their corporate services to re-ject microfilm out of hand. This attitude is marked by such an abiding fear of the conversion process that explanations of potential benefits and economies fall on deaf ears and are resisted until a competitor gains a decisive advantage.

Microfilm systems usually are not practical when the data is constantly changing or the user must interact with the data base. Serving many peo-ple with microfilm requires the strategic placement of many microfilm readers throughout the user organization and the distribution of many copies of the data base. Updating the film to incorporate changes can be accomplished only by the creation of new film. Further, the analyses of large and small computer installations have shown that the minimum page-count volumes must be substantial in order to overcome initially higher fixed costs.

Some of the real-time problems have been alleviated recently by the introduction of film monitors that provide an early inspection of film out-put. The Quantor 100N, an on-line recorder announced only in May 1971, has further advanced the art with a built-in wet-film processor that delivers the first dry film within 12 minutes after system start. A film monitor in the console panel itself permits immediate examination of the film. For real-time systems demanding even faster interaction with the data base, recourse should be made to interactive CRT displays, which can immedi-ately monitor the computer output data. For some unfortunate reason this technique has received extremely limited use to date, but neverthe-less it is a specific solution to the interaction problem.

Users have also experienced problems in training personnel to operate the various phases of a complete COM system, since filming, film develop-ing, and film duplication are new skills that are different from those re-quired of computer operators.

Other disadvantages include the fact that film cannot be written upon, and that the film output of the COM recorder must be constantly checked for image clarity and optical alignment. Moreover, the COM recorder is poorly adapted to applications involving short reports, owing to long job-setup times between runs, or to business applications such as monthly in-voices that require hard-copy output.

Furthermore, microfilm is not a good medium for browsing or multiple-page comparison. Although microimages can be retrieved more readily than paper documents when they are incorporated into a formal system, the material to be filmed must in any case be carefully prepared and or-ganized with appropriate file guides, codes, or indexes. Quite a serious limitation of microfilm readers is their inconvenience to wearers of bifocal glasses. A more general shortcoming is the lack of a cursor or other refer-ence device to return the reader to a specified place after an interruption.

The chief intrinsic obstacle to COM is price—not only the price of COM, but of the entire micrographics field, including readers and reader-print-ers, film processors and duplicators, cameras, and terminals. A possible exception is the price of film. A clarification of this point is perhaps desir-able. It should be obvious that if no COM installation ever justified its promise of economies, the industry would have expired long ago. On the other hand, it should be equally apparent that if no installation had ever failed to justify itself, the long anticipated volume-explosion of the industry certainly would have happened by now. As general as these observations are, they still imply some kind of operational crossover, with profitability lying on one side and disappointment on the other.

Indeed, the experience so far has been this: If monthly report page output is sufficiently high (roughly 100,000 pages or more), or if dupli-cation needs are extensive (say, seven or more of each page), or if the re-quired distribution is extensive and involves long distances, or if there is a suitable mix of all these factors and only moderate need of hard copies (paper reproductions), then the economic advantage of a COM installation over one using impact printers will be controlling. When a satisfactory mix of these conditions does not obtain, the cost of COM in any form (in-house or service bureau) will be prohibitive. Obviously, there will be a gray area somewhere in between these poles for which the advisability of converting to microfilm is questionable.

In view of the slower-than-expected growth of the industry, one might infer that the set of installations for which COM would be advantageous is similarly smaller than supposed. These considerations may help explain why some observers have called for a $20,000 COM. They at least imply that every downward break in prices, not only of the microfilmer but of the system accessories as well, should create a new market segment for which COM recording is preferable to impact printing.

The disappointment due to the sluggish acceptance of COM should not obscure certain positive facts. First, COM technology has continued its slow but pertinacious advance in the face of a retrenched economy that has lowered production generally. Second, the underlying social and commercial pressures that have produced an ever greater demand for printed and graphical output are still potent. Their influences alone will gradually impel more and more establishments into micrographics and COM. Third, the impact of real estate and taxation should not be overlooked as still another force dictating a conversion to microfilm. Even now, floor-space requirements of major insurance companies are so immense that the saving of space effected by COM is extremely important, especially in large cities. This ante is raised further for insurance companies that are taxed for the space they occupy. Fourth, recent innovations in marketing techniques, as represented by usage plans that meter output in order to charge users for actual production instead of imposing a flat rental, promise to become still another source of operational savings. Finally, the trend of basic COM recorder prices is definitely downward. Altogether, these considerations leave no room to doubt the worth of COM recording or to doubt that the industry will expand steadily for many years to come. Only the rate of growth can be questioned—whether this rate is to continue, slow down, or eventually accelerate cannot be forecast, but the evidence is that the signposts of success are in view, not failure.

SYSTEM CONSIDERATIONS

Of a total micrographics system, COM is only one component. Thus, when a user opts for COM, he also makes a decision to abandon established office routine. It is unfair to make COM bear the entire burden of the conversion; yet, to the user, the cost of a printed frame embraces the installation and operational cost of the entire system. In many real-life situations this cost will surpass that of impact printers. Lowering the price of the recorder is not enough; other system components are equally cost-critical. These components and the role they play are depicted in Figure 1-1.

The most variable element of a COM system is the reader and reader-printer facility. If there is only one unit, installation cost is minimized, but then employees will waste time so that the effective cost per report-page mounts. On the other hand, for each added unit, the effective cost of a

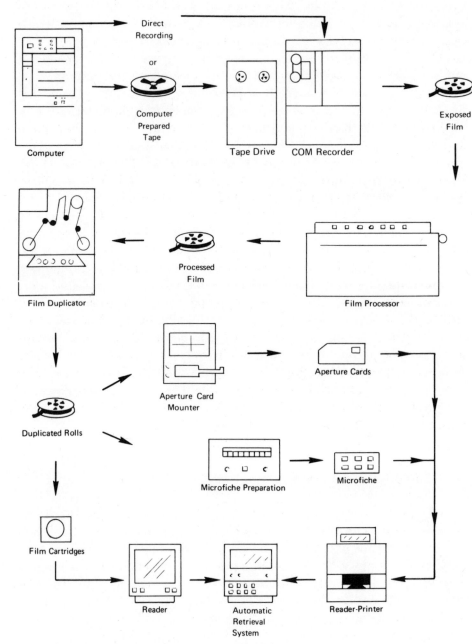

Fig. 1-1.   A typical COM system.

report page also goes up. Not to be overlooked is the expense of producing hard copies of the film. Unfortunately, there is often excessive copying because most people prefer to work with paper rather than film. It should be evident that a substantial reduction in the combined cost of viewers and paper copy can change a marginal situation to one that justifies COM.

Reduction Ratios, Film Sizes, and Microformats

Originally, microfilming employed 35-mm film exclusively at a reduction ratio of about 8X. As optical power improved, higher reduction factors were used to compress more images on the film, i.e., to utilize a given length of film more economically. When a reduction factor of 14X could be achieved without undue loss of detail, document-size images could be imprinted on 16-mm film so that, with film held vertically, the images followed consecutively from top to bottom (cine mode). When reduction factors of 18X and greater were attained, images could be oriented so that, with film held horizontally, the images followed consecutively from edge to edge (comic mode).

With these higher reduction ratios, the use of 16mm film has expanded and gradually supplanted 35-mm film. Most new systems are adopting a reduction ratio of 24X, but virtually all ratios over 14X have been used. Recently, higher reduction factors have been appearing, with 42X dominant. Tables 5-1 and 5-2 disclose the resulting drop in cost per report page when 42X is employed to pack more frames on a roll of film.

When images are recorded one-up, i.e., a single frame across the film at a time, more of the film is left blank at a higher reduction factor than at a lower one. A more efficient technique would be to record two-up, i.e., two frames side by side across the width of the film. For the same number of frames along the length of the film, the total number is doubled and the cost per report page for material is halved. Since the two-up process demands lateral movement and rigid control over the photo-optical system, it is logical to exploit this control with a universal camera as standard or optional equipment. These cameras are so named because they can record on any size film, i.e., 16, 35, 70, or 105-mm, and can photograph laterally as well as longitudinally. In view of these capabilities, the cameras are relatively expensive.

At the 1970 Fall Joint Computer Conference, new single-purpose cameras were displayed (such as a Vought cameras, Computer Equipment Corporation), intended exclusively for 105-mm microfiche applications. Such cameras, without all the universal options, will be less expensive but quite adequate if greater flexibility is not required.

The basic optics technique still standard in most roll-film recorders

today executes the following sequence: Light from images formed on a
CRT screen passes through a half-silver mirror to a camera. When the entire image has been completed, a transparent-form overlay is flashed by a
strobe light to the mirror and reflected to the camera and superposed on
the CRT image; the composite image is then focused by a lens onto the
film. A motor then advances the film to the next recording position. Such
cameras print a series of single frames along the film length in either cine
(top edge to bottom) or comic (left edge to right) mode.

In order to imprint frames across the film width, whether in a two-up
format on 16- or 35-mm film or many columns on 4 x 6-inch fiche (105-
mm film), the step-and-repeat action of a universal camera is needed. Now
the lens is moved along the film in discrete steps, row by row, until the
last frame is recorded, whereupon the camera returns to its starting position and a motor precisely increments the film into position for the next
column. System-logic generating commands in response to the controlling
program governs the entire sequence. This procedure is called *vertical
pagination*.

PROGRAMMING CONSIDERATIONS

The programming situation in the COM industry is improved but still
fairly confused. In the past year, CalComp, DatagraphiX, Kodak, Beta
Instruments, and Memorex have stressed compatibility between their recorders and either tapes or interfaces designed to operate with a standard
impact printer. Sometimes line-printer simulators are provided to adapt
tapes formatted for the popular IBM 1403 printer to the particular COM.
All COM's can accept the IBM 729 class of tape drives, but the actual tape
drives used are selected by the company and integrated within the COM
cabinet. Most COM's are also compatible with other IBM tape formats.

Nevertheless, the special programs to define tabbing, character size,
font selection, character rotation, character intensity, features such as
windowing, translation intermixing of graphics and printing, and so on,
must be programmed locally, often by means of a patch panel or a job
control card, although the more intricate features must be entered in
memory. In this last instance the COM system must include a processor.
With respect to the problem of reformatting tape to harmonize with a
particular COM recorder, the manufacturer will usually provide an appropriate software package. One need only ensure that the specifications of
both the output channel (or interface) commands and the spacing commands assumed by the software actually do apply. Of course there is still
no such thing as a universal program for reformatting all tapes. More manu-

facturers than before are also supplying subroutine packages for the intricate control functions, but these have to be linked with the primary routines of the user, who should also recognize that system debugging is usually a critical matter. Thus, he should be prepared to cope with it.

COM SERVICE BUREAU

An inseparable part of the problem concerning the advisability of converting to COM is whether to patronize a service bureau instead of acquiring in-house facilities. For medium monthly report-page volumes the sensible answer might be: service bureau, yes; in-house, no. A careful cost analysis such as the one performed by the AUERBACH Technical Evaluation Service will explain why. Savings really do not preponderate until the monthly, original page-volume climbs to about 100,000. Other industry sources indicate an even higher crossover figure, but these analyses may antedate recent COM price reductions. One should recognize that the case for COM grows stronger as duplication requirements increase. Similarly, savings rapidly accumulate as distribution of duplicates widens, and the report-page threshold of interest in COM becomes lower in this case as well. In these two instances and many more, nevertheless, recourse to a service bureau might still be preferable. The reason is that there is a surprisingly great range of report output over which the high operating volume of the service bureau enables it to deliver printed frames at a lower cost than they could be produced in-house.

Another consideration is the complications that inevitably arise during the course of any conversion procedure, and conversion to microfilm is hardly an exception. Film recording, film processing, film duplication, and film packaging are usually treacherous to EDP personnel until the disciplines are mastered. Working with a competent service bureau and gaining the benefit of its experience can facilitate the educational process. Planning of the retrieval system alone normally calls for outside consultation. Whether the service bureau is utilized or not, a thoughtful conversion program is decidedly important.

There are approximately 150 COM service bureaus throughout the United States. As a group they have recently experienced a high failure rate primarily because anticipated business growth has failed to materialize. Contributing to this condition were the unwillingness of prospective customers to try microfilm and the intense competition for sales to those people willing to try. Major application areas for service bureaus include billing, payroll, customer histories, credit information, accounts receivable, inventories, and bank statement summaries.

The average COM service bureau is filming some 7 hours per day and has between 20 to 50 customers, with more than 50 percent of these customers filming less than 4 hours per week. The result is that less than 30 percent of the service bureaus surveyed are profitable. Furthermore, they often require three years to break even.

SYSTEM COMPONENTS AND OPERATION

Cameras

Universal cameras usually have interchangeable lens assemblies, with reduction ratios of 24X and 42X now predominating. Changeover to a different film format is effected by resetting control panel switches, as specified by the programmer, and changing the lens whenever necessary.

The DatagraphiX universal camera and the previously mentioned cameras need no shutter, since exposure of the film can be limited to the unblanking time of the cathode-ray tube. A distinctive feature of the Charactron® tube* employed by DatagraphiX is a character-forming stencil in its electron-gun assembly. In addition to the normal recording mode, the DatagraphiX camera can record in the zigzag mode, i.e., in one direction along one column and in the opposite direction along the next, or in the slew-right mode, in which the recording order is always the reverse of the established normal sequence.

A recently introduced camera, the Model DMF-2 DisplayMate of Terminal Data Corporation, holds the optical system fixed while moving film transversely across the lens as well as longitudinally. A stepper motor controls the longitudinal increments and a high-speed servomotor advances the film transversely. When filming 16- or 35-mm film in the linear (one-up) mode, the servomotor increments the frames. Film formats are changed by introducing a different format-control disk within the camera unit and resetting control switches. A variation of this camera especially designed for Kodak microfilmers is known as the VERSAFORM®.†

Film Output

Microfiche

A microfiche is a rectangular sheet of film containing microimages recorded in rows or columns and photographed at reduction ratios from about 18X to 42X. As previously indicated, COM systems have adopted

---

*Charactron is a registered trade name of the DatagraphiX Corp.

†The name VERSAFORM is registered by Kodak.

105-mm film, and the corresponding fiche size is approximately 4 x 6 inches (105 x 148.75 mm). The dominant fiche size in the past was 3¼ x 7⅜ inches (standard tab-card dimensions), but 6 x 8-inch fiche have been produced as well. The COM film output has also been mounted in aperture cards and jackets. Thus, at one time or another, COM has been represented by all the popular microforms. Figure 1-2 illustrates a popular microfiche at a reduction of 24X. Titling will be explained in Chapter 3.

Ultrafiche

A new format now available with exceptional film utilization and page-cost economy is called ultrafiche. As defined by the National Microfilm As-

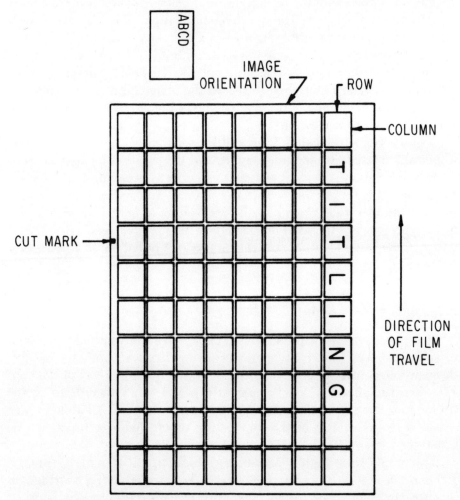

Fig. 1-2.   Typical microfiche format at 24X reduction.

sociation, an ultrafiche is a microformat holding images reduced 100X or more with respect to the original. Two reduction ratios are used at present, 120X and 150X. A serious disadvantage of ultrafiche is its vulnerability to damage. Even a tiny scratch severely damages the small image. The NCR ultrafiche is placed in a laminated sandwich that protects the film but precludes its use for duplication.

FILM PREPARATION AND USE

Exposure Techniques

Certain basic exposure techniques and classes of film are commonly used in the COM industry. The most common output film is a silver halide type that is exposed to visible light from a CRT. An example is Kodak Dacomatic, which can capture fine image detail but is still fairly inexpensive. Usually, a full page is printed or a full graphic display is generated on the CRT before a camera is strobed to record the image on film. If duplicates are required, the original film must contain a higher order of detail than if intended solely for viewing.

Two special silver halide films call for separate consideration. One is a specially treated film provided by the 3M Corporation for its EBR. Subsequent discussion will point out that exposure is accomplished by electrons impinging on the film within the CRT envelope. After removal from the CRT, the film is developed by the application of heat. The second unusual type, which is found in the Memorex 1603 printer, reacts to infrared energy rather than to either visible or ultraviolet radiation. It is processed in the usual way.

Processing Requirements

Except for EBR film, exposed silver halide film must eventually be taken to a film processor, where it is submerged in chemical solutions and fed through rollers to exit completely developed at the other end of the tub. This disadvantage of wet development explains why either diazo or vesicular film supplants silver halide film in duplication. Another potent reason is the lower cost of the duplicating types. (Refer to discussion in Chapter 5.)

The output from both processor and duplicator is 16-mm, 35-mm, or 105-mm roll film. For storage, the roll may be inserted into a cartridge or cassette, cut to form microfiche, or inserted into an aperture card mounter where each frame is cut and individually placed on a tab card. Hard copy may be obtained via a reader/printer. or information may be retrieved visually via a manual reader or automatically via a retrieval system.

Viewing and Printing

An organization must have enough microfilm viewing and printing devices to permit convenient use of the microfilm produced by the COM installation. One of the roadblocks to acceptance of the COM technology is that the user must go to the reader location to obtain desired data from film, but once employees become familiar with microfilm and a sufficient number of readers are deployed, the medium is usually accepted. Until the adjustment is made, however, adverse employee reactions may present serious problems. The importance of user education cannot be overstated.

From an economic standpoint the advantage of a COM system is determined by the overall system cost weighed against displaced costs. For this reason, the cost of the COM recorder, personnel, and other equipment, such as viewers and viewer/printers, must be considered. Because users may need many microfilm readers and reader/printers, of which the monthly rentals are between $50 and $60, their cost may be the determining factor in a decision regarding COM.

Although the wages paid to operators of COM equipment, processors, and duplicators are nominal, some skill is required of the operator and, above all, he must be reliable and reasonably devoted to his responsibilities. Since such people are not plentiful, training costs must be included in the original capitalization. Training is doubly important in that it is a selection process as well as an instructional one.

Many COM manufacturers offer a line of accessory equipment, such as readers and reader/printers, along with their COM recorders to facilitate the assembly of complete and compatible systems that eliminate interface problems. However, Memorex is the first company to offer substantially reduced prices for adequate readers and reader/printers ($15 and $20, respectively). This low price range is partly attributable to a special easy-to-handle film cassette that snaps into place in equipment designed to handle only such cassettes. Quantor has also announced a lower-priced reader for use in document retrieval. The Model 300, which rents for as little as $36 monthly on a three-year lease, can scan film electronically at speeds of over 100 frames per second.

2. APPLICATIONS AND ACCOMPLISHMENTS OF COM

There are three main types of COM recorders today, as classified by their basic applications:

1. Alphanumeric (nonimpact) printer: produces alphanumeric characters and symbols only according to preconcerted formats; for example, the standard computer printout format consists of 64 lines of 132 characters each. Some printers are restricted to this page structure; others can adjust to different structures, such as 86 lines per frame.

2. Alphanumeric/business graphics: combines alphanumeric printing and labeling with low-precision graphic exhibits, such as bar and circular charts, graphs, and line drawings.

3. High-resolution/graphic arts: executes precision scientific and engineering plots and line drawings, some photocomposition, and similar applications requiring high resolution and exact layout.

Figure 2-1 presents an estimated market distribution of these categories.

In view of the declining prices of alphanumeric printers in an environment of voluminous printouts, Figure 2-1 shows that this market sector enjoys a significant sales potential at present and suggests an opportunity for the first important profits in the history of the industry. On the other hand, the dominant market share of alphanumeric/business graphics proves the presence of demand; thus, if a limited graphics capability could be added to alphanumeric recorders without appreciably increasing cost, demand should be intensified further.

Table 2-1 lists some examples of the main types of COM's.

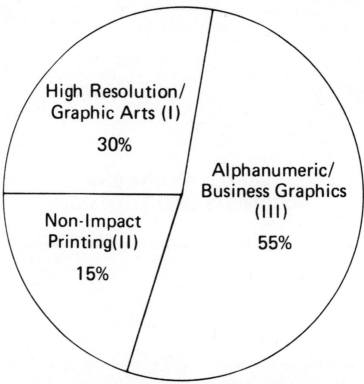

Fig. 2-1.   Distribution of COM recorders by market segment.
(Reprinted from ATES COM report.)

SPECIFIC EXAMPLES

One specific application is demand deposit accounting in the banking industry, for which microfilm is a practical means of distributing large quantities of data to the branches. Other examples include the maintenance of policy histories and insurance claims for insurance companies, listing of automobile registrations, listing of job opportunities for state governments, and recording of fare quotation data for airlines. Representative application areas are listed in Table 2-2.

Figure 2-2 presents a distribution of the major applications according to a recent survey conducted by AUERBACH Info, Inc.

SOME ACCOMPLISHMENTS OF COM INSTALLATIONS

Our surveys have also evoked incidental comments on how various COM installations have paid off:

1. Time saved by a well-organized retrieval system.

2. Time saved by the recording operation as follows: printing accomplished in first shift, overtime charges eliminated; retrieval coding conveniently imprinted; manual operation of microfiche camera avoided; nonprecision drafting functions eliminated by automatic plotting; engineering personnel accommodated sooner; errors in computer programs exposed sooner; similarly, programs improved and expanded sooner through contributions of the most creative personnel as experience revealed needs; the careful programming of details into the operations that prevented their periodic omission by forgetful office personnel. Furthermore, any information actually forgotten would usually be quickly exposed by graphical presentations.

Table 2-1.   Partial List of Three Main COM Types

NAME OF COM	TYPE	APPROX. PRICE, $
Information International FR-80	High-resolution/graphic arts	225,000
Link MS-5000	High-resolution/graphic arts (engineering)	125,000
Beta COM 600, 700°	Alphanumeric/business graphics	130,000 155,000
CalComp 900/835°	Alphanumeric/business graphics	90,000
CalComp 1670 printer/plotter	High-resolution/graphic arts	120,000
University computing 120 printer/plotter	Alphanumeric/business graphics	120,000
DatagraphiX 4020	Alphanumeric/business graphics	155,000
3M Series "F" EBR	Alphanumeric/business graphics	105,000
Ferranti ADE plotter°	Alphanumeric/business graphics	60,000
Peripheral Technology PTI-1300, PTI-2600	Alphanumeric printer	49,750
SEACO Model 401	Alphanumeric printer	39,850
Kodak KOM-80, KOM-90	Alphanumeric printer	63,000† 88,000†
DatagraphiX 4200	Alphanumeric printer‡	49,000§
DatagraphiX 4440	Alphanumeric printer	108,000
Memorex 1603 microfilm printer	Alphanumeric printer‡	44,250
Sequential s/COM-70	Alphanumeric/business graphics	32,850

°Often used in engineering and scientific plotting.
†Does not include price of camera.
‡Intended for on-line operation.
§Including Universal camera.

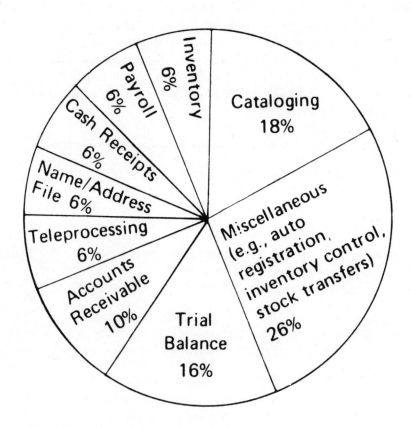

Fig. 2-2.   Distribution of major applications among surveyed users
(excluding service bureaus). (Reprinted from ATES COM report.)

Table 2-2.   Representative Uses for COM

INDUSTRY	APPLICATION AREAS	DISTRIBUTION
Banking	Demand deposit accounting	Branches
Automotive	Parts lists	Suppliers
Airlines	Fare information	Agents
Libraries	Book inventories	Reading rooms
Specialty steel	Item inventories	Warehouses
Mail order	Catalog information	Order takers
Book publishing	Micropublishing	Customers
Engineering	Scientific graphs, engineering drawings	Engineers, technicians
Finance and investment	Charts, graphs, tables general printing	Personnel, clients, government agencies
General commerce and industry	Customer accounts, office records, balance sheets, trial balances, payroll, etc.	Personnel, customers (hard copy), other company divisions
Insurance	Agents' commission statements, agents' digest system, customer statements, check copies retrieval, payroll statements, physicians' records, vendors' records	Agents, personnel, supervisors, branches
Animated movies and scientific sequencing	Advertising, engineering, chemistry, scientific research	Television stations, theaters, laboratories, universities
Education and training films	Education and training	Classrooms and auditoriums

21

3. TECHNOLOGY OF COM

The function of a COM recorder is to convert the coded digital output of a computer into a discernable image and to record the image on microfilm.

All COM systems that display and record computer-generated graphic data also accept alphanumeric data. Computer graphics systems must have software support to exploit the capabilities of the equipment, but implementing the software adds significantly to the cost, since an internal control processor is required. The software and processor are also used to translate a variety of input formats into a specified format of coded alphanumeric character data, graphic vector specifications and control instructions for both. In addition, software control programs translate the computer output into formats required for specific applications.

Since a large number of applications require only alphanumerics, a new type of system was developed, specializing solely in high-speed, reduced-cost alphanumeric recording (a direct competitor to the impact printers). A characteristic of these new alphanumeric printers is the omission of internal control processors and the restriction to one basic input format. Plugboards or job control card readers are substituted for software, however, to provide output formatting commands as required by particular applications. Off line or on line, the alphanumeric printer can then process any tape conforming to its designated input format.

Both alphanumeric and graphic COM systems have a forms-overlay capacity, which consists of a prepared form (usually drawn on a slide according to rigid specifications) that can be superimposed on the computer-generated data. In some of the more elaborate graphic display COM systems, the prescribed forms are stored in the computer memory and electronically overlaid when directed by the controlling program.

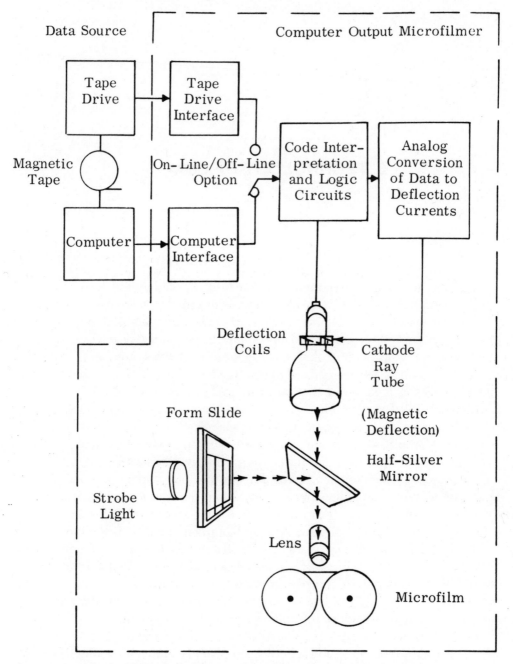

Fig. 3-1.   System components of COM, CRT imaging.

COMPONENTS OF A COM SYSTEM

An alphanumeric COM system consists of the following basic components (see Fig. 3-1):

1. Mainframe computer: generates the data to be displayed.
2. Direct input source: the computer interface in on-line operation or a magnetic-tape transport and an appropriate interface in off-line operation.
3. Code interpretation and logic circuits: interpret digitized code of input data, generate required signals for character generation or formation of graphics, drive analog conversion section, and develop signals for control of photo-optical devices.
4. Analog conversion circuits: convert digital input from logic circuits into deflection currents (voltages if electrostatic deflection is used) that position the characters, symbols, or vectors appropriately on the display screen.
5. Cathode-ray tube: forms the proper image.
6. Strobe light and forms slide: at the instant signaled by the logic circuits, the strobe light is flashed so that the forms-slide image is superimposed on the computer data imaged onto the film from the CRT.
7. Half-silver mirror: passes enough light from the CRT and deflects enough light from the forms slide to project both images onto the film.
8. Camera: records the images on microfilm or microfiche.

The LED principle will be taken up later. When the COM system has an internal processor, it is placed between the interface and code interpretation functions.

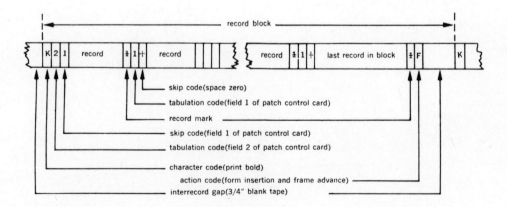

Fig. 3-2.   Typical COM record block with control codes on magnetic tape.

PAGE STRUCTURING

A standard computer printout page consists of 64 lines of 132 characters per line. All alphanumeric recorders produce page frames conforming with this structure, and many offer alternative formats as well.

The positions of plotted shapes, indentions, intensity, character size and font, orientation, and other display parameters are controlled by a combination of internal COM circuits and commands provided by the digital input stream. The digital input is programmed in the computer to provide specific directions for the end of a line (equivalent to carriage return), the end of a page (frame advance), various types of indentions and skips,

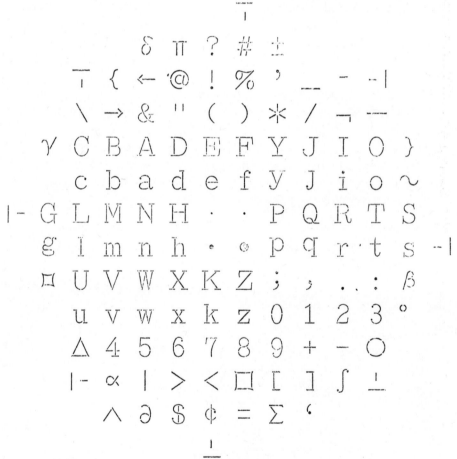

Fig. 3-3. (a) DatagraphiX 4060 character set (with serifs);

various character sizes and display intensities (when permitted by the machine), and so forth.

Each COM has the equivalent of an instruction set of nonprinting characters, which are uniquely interpreted by the COM to initiate the control functions. On magnetic tapes formatted for a COM, a record is defined as a line of data, and a record block usually constitutes one frame. An example of a complete COM record block with interspersed control codes is illustrated in Figure 3-2. The format illustrated is generally consistent with the formatting requirements of most manufacturers' equipment.

Once the digital input is reconstructed by the COM into visual images on the fact of a CRT, the displayed images are photographed by a microfilm camera. The data is literally written across the face of the CRT by the

$$
\begin{array}{cccccccccccc}
 & & & & & & \overline{} & & & & & \\
 & & & \delta & \pi & ? & \# & \pm & & & & \\
 & & \{ & \leftarrow & @ & ! & \% & ' & \_ & - & & \\
 & \backslash & \rightarrow & \& & " & (&) & \ast & / & \neg & - & \\
\gamma & C & B & A & D & E & F & Y & J & I & \acute{O} & \} \\
 & c & b & a & d & e & f & y & J & \dot{\imath} & o & \sim \\
\vdash & G & L & M & N & H & \cdot & \cdot & P & Q & R & T & S \\
g & I & m & n & h & \bullet & \circledcirc & p & q & r & t & s & -! \\
\rtimes & U & V & W & X & K & Z & ; & , & . & : & \beta \\
 & u & v & w & x & k & z & 0 & 1 & 2 & 3 & \degree \\
 & \triangle & 4 & 5 & 6 & 7 & 8 & 9 & \div & - & \bigcirc \\
 & \propto & | & > & < & \square & [&] & \int & \pounds \\
 & \wedge & \partial & \$ & \cent & = & \Sigma & ' \\
 & & & & & \overline{} & & & & & &
\end{array}
$$

(b) sans serif.

electron beam in the desired page format and is photographed at the writing speed. The writing speed varies among the various COM's. Most are bound by both the input tape rate, which characteristically varies from 30,000 to 120,000 characters per second, and the frame advance rate.

Examples of character fonts and symbols that are printed by various COM's appear in Figures 3-3 through 3-5.

Fig. 3-4.   Beta COM 600 character set (sans serif).

OPERATIONAL MODE

The COM recorders can operate on line with a computer and thereby process the generated data as it is produced, or they can operate off line from a magnetic-tape transport. A typical COM configuration, showing alternative on-line and off-line operations, was presented in Figure 3-1.

On-Line Operation

Interface electronics for decoding on-line computer output and forming displays are simpler than those required for off-line operation, and avoid the substantial cost of a tape transport Thus, on-line recorders designed for a specific class of computer systems such as the IBM/360 cost less to produce than off-line systems with comparable components. Furthermore, on-line operation is carried out in one step with no intervening time delay and extra handling requirements.

On-line COM recorders match or exceed many computer output speeds. For those cases where the processor is faster, the computer interface usually has a multiple channel capability so that additional COM recorders can

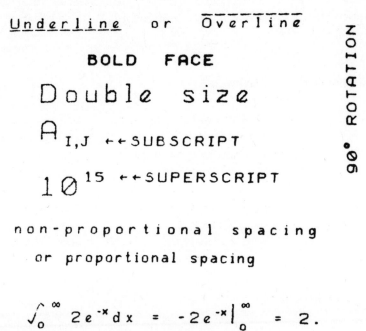

Fig. 3-5.   Character structures and orientations.

be added. The final COM configuration would be less extensive than an equivalent impact printer configuration, in view of the higher COM throughput rates.

A disadvantage of COM on-line operation in relation to paper is that film output must await processing before it can be viewed. Thus, a mistake in the computer output would not be known until later, and the computer program would have to be rerun. If the COM operation itself were faulty, that situation also would not be revealed until later. Thus, checking and rerun procedures are extremely important.

Off-Line Operation

This mode of operation also delays production of a readable image. In addition, a two-step sequence is required to produce the film: (1) recording the computer output on magnetic tape, and (2) later transferring the magnetic-tape data to the COM recorder for processing and micro-filming. Although the second step involves the expense of a tape trans-port, two advantages accrue. First, the computer can output at the higher speeds of a tape drive; second, only the tape transport needs to be rerun in the event of error. However, since data transfer and decoding from tape to the COM recorder are slower than from a computer interface, the throughput rate of an off-line model is somewhat less than that of a com-parable on-line device.

IMAGE FORMATION TECHNIQUES

COM recorders now on the market employ three different image for-mation techniques. The cathode-ray tube (CRT) method, by far the most widely used, generates an image on the face of the CRT, which is trans-ferred to film by a camera. The second technique is the 3M Company electron-beam recording (EBR) procedure, which uses the electron beam of the CRT to expose a special type of film. The third technique, in some respects the most promising approach, employs the light-emitting diode (LED) array with or without a fiber-optics adjunct to form alphanumeric characters on a matrix of diodes, a line at a time.

CRT Microfilm Recording

In this process, digital data produced by the computer is transformed into analog signals that form an image on a moderately persistent phos-phorescent screen. After a frame of data has been generated, a camera photographs a combined image of the data and a selected custom form. Although not yet installed in any COM on the market, optical systems may eventually photograph one line at a time or even each character as it is formed. Refer again to Figure 3-1.

Image formation on the CRT is preeminent in resolution and ease of adjustment, and is also reasonable in cost. Primarily because of its resolv-ing power, this technology is essential in the field of high-resolution/graphic arts recording. Moreover, no other method can produce a color display, for which a demand is expected in the future.

On the other hand, the CRT has some detrimental characteristics. In terms of the precision and stability requirements of COM recording, it is inherently an unstable, nonlinear device. Its spot size varies slightly across the screen, causing astigmatism. Both spot size and location tend to vary in response to small voltage and circuit parameter deviations, results of aging, operational stress, and environmental changes. Essentially an ana-

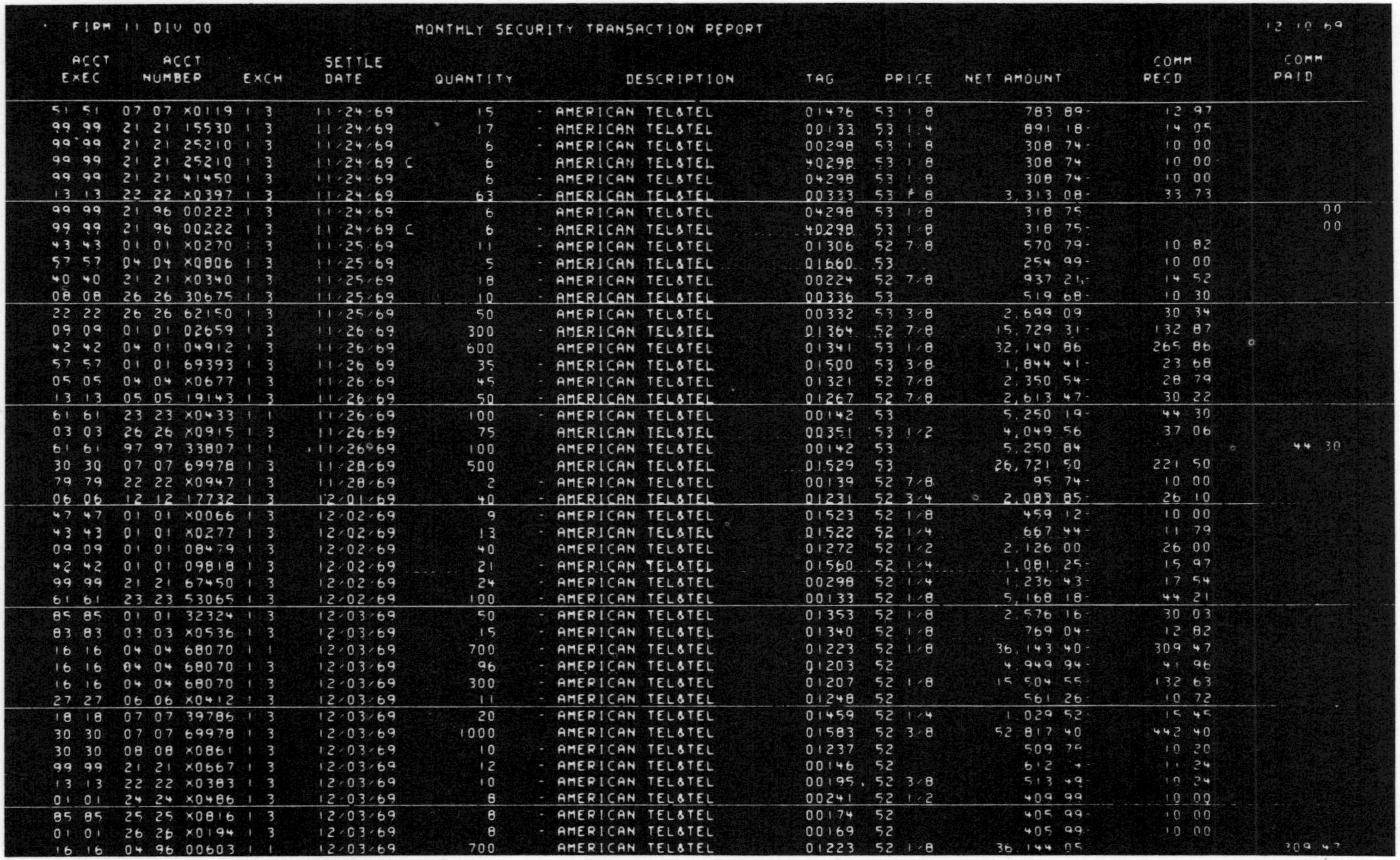

FIRM 11 DIV 00 MONTHLY SECURITY TRANSACTION REPORT 12 10 69

ACCT EXEC	ACCT NUMBER	EXCH	SETTLE DATE	QUANTITY	DESCRIPTION	TAG	PRICE	NET AMOUNT	COMM RECD	COMM PAID
51 51	07 07 X0119	1 3	11/24/69	15	- AMERICAN TEL&TEL	01476	53 1/8	783 89-	12 97	
99 99	21 21 15530	1 3	11/24/69	17	- AMERICAN TEL&TEL	00133	53 1/4	891 18-	14 05	
99 99	21 21 25210	1 3	11/24/69	6	- AMERICAN TEL&TEL	00298	53 1/8	308 74-	10 00	
99 99	21 21 25210	1 3	11/24/69 C	6	AMERICAN TEL&TEL	40298	53 1/8	308 74	10 00-	
99 99	21 21 41450	1 3	11/24/69	6	- AMERICAN TEL&TEL	04298	53 1/8	308 74-	10 00	
13 13	22 22 X0397	1 3	11/24/69	63	- AMERICAN TEL&TEL	00333	53 1/8	3,313 08-	33 73	
99 99	21 96 00222	1 3	11/24/69	6	AMERICAN TEL&TEL	04298	53 1/8	318 75		00
99 99	21 96 00222	1 3	11/24/69 C	6	- AMERICAN TEL&TEL	40298	53 1/8	318 75-		00
43 43	01 01 X0270	1 3	11/25/69	11	- AMERICAN TEL&TEL	01306	52 7/8	570 79-	10 82	
57 57	04 04 X0806	1 3	11/25/69	5	- AMERICAN TEL&TEL	01660	53	254 99-	10 00	
40 40	21 21 X0340	1 3	11/25/69	18	- AMERICAN TEL&TEL	00224	52 7/8	937 21-	14 52	
08 08	26 26 30675	1 3	11/25/69	10	- AMERICAN TEL&TEL	00336	53	519 68-	10 30	
22 22	26 26 62150	1 3	11/25/69	50	AMERICAN TEL&TEL	00332	53 3/8	2,699 09	30 34	
09 09	01 01 02659	1 3	11/26/69	300	- AMERICAN TEL&TEL	01364	52 7/8	15,729 31-	132 87	
42 42	04 01 04912	1 3	11/26/69	600	AMERICAN TEL&TEL	01341	53 1/8	32,140 86	265 86	
57 57	01 01 69393	1 3	11/26/69	35	- AMERICAN TEL&TEL	01500	53 3/8	1,844 41-	23 68	
05 05	04 04 X0677	1 3	11/26/69	45	- AMERICAN TEL&TEL	01321	52 7/8	2,350 54-	28 79	
13 13	05 05 19143	1 3	11/26/69	50	- AMERICAN TEL&TEL	01267	52 7/8	2,613 47-	30 22	
61 61	23 23 X0433	1 1	11/26/69	100	- AMERICAN TEL&TEL	00142	53	5,250 19-	44 30	
03 03	26 26 X0915	1 3	11/26/69	75	AMERICAN TEL&TEL	00351	53 1/2	4,049 56	37 06	
61 61	97 97 33807	1 1	11/26/69	100	AMERICAN TEL&TEL	00142	53	5,250 84		44 30
30 30	07 07 69978	1 3	11/28/69	500	AMERICAN TEL&TEL	01529	53	26,721 50	221 50	
79 79	22 22 X0947	1 3	11/28/69	2	- AMERICAN TEL&TEL	00139	52 7/8	95 74-	10 00	
06 06	12 12 17732	1 3	12/01/69	40	- AMERICAN TEL&TEL	01231	52 3/4	2,083 85-	26 10	
47 47	01 01 X0066	1 3	12/02/69	9	- AMERICAN TEL&TEL	01523	52 1/8	459 12-	10 00	
43 43	01 01 X0277	1 3	12/02/69	13	- AMERICAN TEL&TEL	01522	52 1/4	667 44-	11 79	
09 09	01 01 08479	1 3	12/02/69	40	AMERICAN TEL&TEL	01272	52 1/2	2,126 00	26 00	
42 42	01 01 09818	1 3	12/02/69	21	- AMERICAN TEL&TEL	01560	52 1/4	1,081 25-	15 97	
99 99	21 21 67450	1 3	12/02/69	24	- AMERICAN TEL&TEL	00298	52 1/4	1,236 43-	17 54	
61 61	23 23 53065	1 3	12/02/69	100	- AMERICAN TEL&TEL	00133	52 1/8	5,168 18-	44 21	
85 85	01 01 32324	1 3	12/03/69	50	- AMERICAN TEL&TEL	01353	52 1/8	2,576 16-	30 03	
83 83	03 03 X0536	1 3	12/03/69	15	- AMERICAN TEL&TEL	01340	52 1/8	769 04-	12 82	
16 16	04 04 68070	1 1	12/03/69	700	- AMERICAN TEL&TEL	01223	52 1/8	36,143 40-	309 47	
16 16	04 04 68070	1 3	12/03/69	96	- AMERICAN TEL&TEL	01203	52	4,949 94-	41 96	
16 16	04 04 68070	1 3	12/03/69	300	- AMERICAN TEL&TEL	01207	52 1/8	15,504 55-	132 63	
27 27	06 06 X0412	1 3	12/03/69	11	- AMERICAN TEL&TEL	01248	52	561 26-	10 72	
18 18	07 07 39786	1 3	12/03/69	20	- AMERICAN TEL&TEL	01459	52 1/4	1,029 52-	15 45	
30 30	07 07 69978	1 3	12/03/69	1000	AMERICAN TEL&TEL	01583	52 3/8	52,817 40	442 40	
30 30	08 08 X0861	1 3	12/03/69	10	- AMERICAN TEL&TEL	01237	52	509 7[illegible]	10 20	
99 99	21 21 X0667	1 3	12/03/69	12	- AMERICAN TEL&TEL	00146	52	612 [illegible]	11 24	
13 13	22 22 X0383	1 3	12/03/69	10	- AMERICAN TEL&TEL	00195	52 3/8	513 49-	10 24	
01 01	24 24 X0486	1 3	12/03/69	8	- AMERICAN TEL&TEL	00241	52 1/2	409 99	10 00	
85 85	25 25 X0816	1 3	12/03/69	8	- AMERICAN TEL&TEL	00174	52	405 99-	10 00	
01 01	26 26 X0194	1 3	12/03/69	8	- AMERICAN TEL&TEL	00169	52	405 99-	10 00	
16 16	04 96 00603	1 1	12/03/69	700	AMERICAN TEL&TEL	01223	52 1/8	36,144 05		309 47

Fig. 3-6. Typical page of data as viewed on Quantor 300 display station.

log device, the CRT requires that the digital information supplied by the computer be translated into analog deflection voltages. Stabilization and linearity correction of considerable refinement also contribute to the cost of the device.

An example of the excellent print quality obtainable from alphanumeric recorders today appears in Figure 3-6.

Electron Beam Recording

The technique used exclusively by its developer in the 3M Company series "F" electron beam recorder is portrayed in Figure 3-7. In this process the CRT electron beam writes directly on special 3M dry-silver film passing through the interior of the CRT enclosure under vacuum. Thus, light is not used in the film-exposure process. After exposure, the film can be transferred directly to a companion film processor, where it is developed through the application of heat and emerges ready for viewing. As shown in Figure 3-7, a forms-insertion system is used to supply a forms overlay.

The electron beam recorder is a special kind of CRT. The distinguishing concept of the EBR method is the passage of film into and out of the CRT

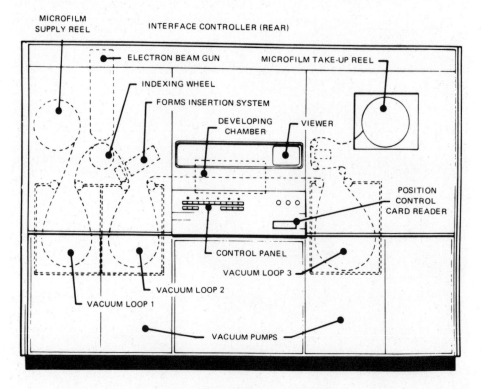

Fig. 3-7.   Electron beam recording.

envelope. Direct impact of the CRT electron beam on specially prepared film instead of on a conventional phosphorescent screen causes exposure of the image traced by the beam. Interviews with EBR users indicate that the developed film is sensitive to subsequent applications of heat. Except for this problem, operation of the EBR system is reported to be satisfactory.

LED Microfilm Recording

Light-emitting diodes, coupled with fiber-optics light conductors, create the alphanumeric output image in the Memorex 1603. A second system, the Sequential Information Systems S/COM-70, also utilizes the LED principle, but omits fiber optics.

The Memorex technique is illustrated in Figure 3-8. Control signals are provided by a character-buffer translation matrix to a bank of 140 diodes. Fiber-optics strands attached to each diode conduct infrared light emitted by the diodes to a fiber-optics assembly. The strands terminate at the assembly face in a compact horizontal row of 132 successive 5 x 7 ma-

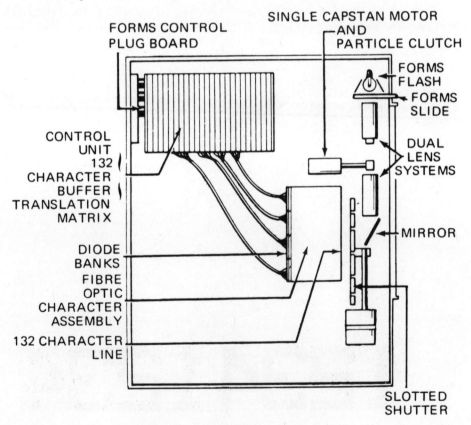

Fig. 3-8.   Fiber-optics recording.

trices; hence, there are 4620 conductors in all. When character data signals are received, certain diodes are illuminated selectively by circuit action, and the tips of their attached strands glow at the assembly face.

Since each character matrix consists of 35 elements, only 4 characters can be constructed at a time from the 140 diodes. It can also be seen that each diode must occupy the same relative position in 33 consecutive sets of 4 character matrices to compose the total of 132 at the assembly face; hence, each diode must be attached to 33 fiber-optics strands. A succession of 33 identical sets of 4 characters therefore glow at the assembly face at one time.

A rotating disk with 12 slots at 30-degree intervals is synchronized to place one of its slots in position to pass light from the first three characters. See Figure 3-9. The slot width is restricted to accept light from only three characters so that, as the shutter rotates, light from the fourth character—rather than from the first character of the next set—will be transmitted. Light passing through the slot falls upon a mirror, which reflects it to a lens system and upon 16-mm film at the start of a character line.

After a full line has been exposed, the film is advanced one character line, and the preceding cycle is repeated. After 64 lines are recorded, the

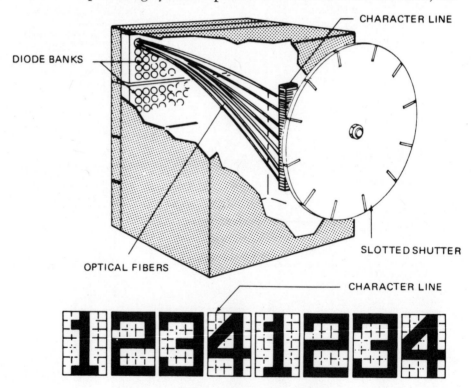

Fig. 3-9.   Memorex character generator.

film is indexed 14 lines to the start of the next frame. In this manner a standard computer printout of 64 lines, 132 characters per line, is compressed into one frame on film. Thus, the Memorex 1603 printer has no camera in the conventional sense. The time required to print a line and index the film to the next character line is 6 msec, of which 3 msec are expended on printing and 3 msec on film indexing. If the machine were to operate continuously, therefore, 10,000 lines per minutes would be printed.

Pulldown requires only 28 msec, since film movement during this process can be accelerated to average 2 msec per line. A simple calculation puts the throughput at 145 pages per minute. At present, 16-mm film is the only output medium of the 1603 microfilmer, and cine mode is the only recorded format. It sells for $44,250.

Other Systems

The Sequential s/COM-70 will dispense with the fiber-optics light conductors and array the diodes in a single compact row of 924 elements. This quantity breaks down into 132 sets of seven diodes. If there are always two blank spaces between characters, the horizontal structure of a character must consist of five columns. The vertical character structure of the s/COM comprises 12 rows, but the top 5 are left blank to separate the lines of characters printed on film. Under the impetus of the film-drive system,

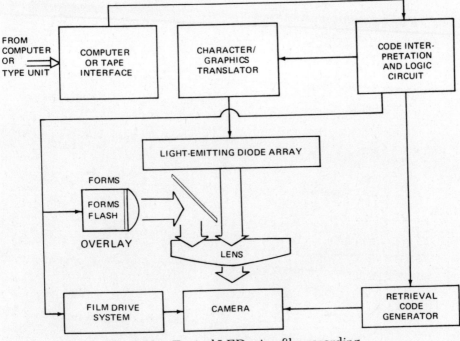

Fig. 3-10. Typical LED microfilm recording.

Fig. 3-11. Alphanumeric printout of sequential systems S/COM-70.

which in turn is controlled by the code interpretation and logic circuits, the film is advanced the five rows, or dot lines, to the top dot line of the character matrix. See Figure 3-10. Again under the control of system logic, the character generator now illuminates those diodes in each of the 132 sets of 7 that are required for the eventual formation of the proper characters (see the printout in Fig. 3-11). That dot line is simultaneously recorded on the film, and the film is precisely advanced to the next dot line. The red light emitted by the diodes passes directly through a lens and into a camera that transfers the sequence of dots to the film. Altogether, the illumination of diodes to form dot lines occurs seven times before the film is again advanced six dot lines to the top of the next character. In this manner characters are constructed from a 5 x 7 matrix by means of no more than a single row of diodes.

It should also be evident that, with the film virtually in continuous motion, the transit of film from one character line to the next is swift, and therefore the effective frame-advance time is quite short. Indeed, Sequential specifies this time at 10 msec maximum. This figure should be compared with 28 msec for the Memorex 1603, 30 msec for the Quantor 100 series microfilm recorder, 60 msec for the SEACO COM recorder Model 401, and 100 msec or more for most of the others. For a given character-generation rate, reducing the frame-advance time from some reference makes the machine appear to be operating at a faster rate than it actually is. This property should probably be traded off for price savings—rather than for higher throughput—by employing slower circuit components, a slower interface, or a slower tape transport. The reason is that price at the present time seems to be the industry's severest deterrent to sales, but even modest operating speeds are adequate for many if not quite all applications. When employed in the same way as the Memorex 1603, the s/COM-70 prints at the continuous rate of 15,000 lines per minute and generates 225 standard frames per minute. This throughput is due in part to short frame-pulldown time (1 msec/character-line).

With the addition of an optional graphics kit, the s/COM-70 will connect dots to plot so-called business graphs.

Like the Memorex 1603, the Sequential s/COM-70 records in cine mode on 16-mm film. By means of its optional universal camera, it can format the standard microfiche on 105-mm film as well, either at a reduction ratio of 24X (80 frames per fiche) or 42X (224 frames per fiche). In addition, the camera is capable of recording on 35-mm and 70-mm film.

Perhaps the outstanding attribute of the s/COM-79 is simplicity. Simple devices are usually inexpensive, and the $32,850 purchase price of the alphanumeric printer is presently the second lowest. The camera is also extremely easy to operate.

It should also be interesting to compare a sample of printed output from the s/com-70, as shown in Figure 3-11, with the Quantor sample in Figure 3-6. Memorex output observed at demonstrations was of equal quality. Light-emitting diodes as an image-forming technique are conceptually similar to the familiar spectacle of images formed on a billboard mosaic of lights that are selectively turned on and off. To be sure, the density of elements in an led array is far greater than that commonly exhibited on billboards.

Owing to the higher luminescence of the diodes compared with crt phosphors, moreover, film sensitivity is even less critical than in crt recorders. This advantage is fortunate in view of the growth difficulty in making extended-red sensitive films as compared to the ease of making view extended-blue film.

Sequential's recorder uses a forms overlay of the same relative size as the diode array. It is reduced through the lens and camera in the same way as the diode image. The Memorex recorder employs a precision forms slide that is focused by a dual lens system and reflected by a mirror onto the film. Note that the larger overlay of the Sequential system does not require precision drawing as the forms slide does. Nevertheless, the tolerance allowed for its position in the recorder is exacting, in order that its image appear in the proper place on the film.

The Quantor 100N microfilm printer employs only 32 photodiodes. A tiny mirror is associated with each diode, and the mirrors are rotated in synchronism by a precision motor so that light from the corresponding diodes is deflected linearly across the width of 16-mm film.

If at regular intervals certain diodes are illuminated for short bursts in accordance with the digital signals received from the host computer, appropriate dots along a horizontal row on the film will be recorded. Clearly, the basic principle of character generation parallels the dot-line technique of the Sequential s/com-70. In particular, after each dot row on the film has received its sequence of recorded dots, the film is indexed to the next dot line and the mirrors are returned to their starting positions.

A major improvement of the Quantor 100N over the other systems is the use of a 7 x 10 matrix structure instead of a 5 x 7. This provision results in excellent print quality and should overcome industry complaints about eye fatigue. The 100N prints only on 16-mm film at the rate of 10,000 lines per minute and formats frames only in cine mode. Its price of $29,995 is the lowest of any alphanumeric printer. Like the s/com-70, the 100N has a limited graphics capability.

The led technique has the advantage of being potentially less expensive, more reliable, and simpler to operate. By construction, the image mosaic is physically stationary and thus needs no electronic stabilizing circuits or analog conversion, as required in crt systems. Focusing adjustments are eliminated, as are the problems of astigmatism and linearity. Hence, many front panel and screwdriver controls typical of CRT recorders are unnecessary. These observations are confirmed by users of the 1603, who have expressed satisfaction with its dependability of performance and simplicity of operation.

Requirements for precision control, however, are not totally eliminated. In the previously described LED systems, film increments must be precisely equal; otherwise an irregular image will be formed on the film. In planning alphanumeric recorders, therefore, the designer may choose linearizing CRT images electronically or controlling the movement of film electromechanically. Of course film movement in a CRT recorder must be also carefully controlled.

Shortcomings of the LED technique include a tendency of the characters to smear because of light persistence, or to be of marginal quality, owing to the limited number of matrix elements. The optical system must merge the dots precisely if the characters are to look smooth. This requirement is generally met satisfactorily.

The Memorex 1603 recorder is currently restricted to alphanumerics. A limited graphics capability will be offered in the Sequential s/COM-70.

Calculations of Throughput

A basic approach will be taken in this problem to illustrate the most representative situations. The applicable equation is

$$N_f = \frac{60,000}{T_t}$$

where: N_f = number of frames per minute

T_t = total time in milliseconds to print frame and arrive at starting position of next frame

Now

$$T_t = n_f t_c + t_f + t_{fo} + n_I t_I$$

where: n_f = number of characters to be printed per frame

t_c = time required to generate a single character in milliseconds

t_f = frame advance time or equivalent

t_{fo} = time in milliseconds to locate and strobe a random form overlay

t_I = time in milliseconds to read inter-record gap

n_I = number of inter-record gaps included in the page-frame format

When a standard page-frame format is printed, n_f is equal to 8448. To determine t_c, one must choose the smaller of the inherent character generation rate of the recorder and the input character transfer rate. Suppose this rate is n_c in characters per second. Then

$$t_c = \frac{1000}{N_c}$$

Sometimes the character generation rate quoted by the manufacturer is an equivalent rate that absorbs the frame-advance time. Then t_f drops out of the equation. Usually, t_1 is neglected in the calculation, but for exact results it should be included. Its value is simply to 1000 times the inter-record gap length in inches/tape-reading speed. It is noted that n_1 does not include the gap following the frame-advanced command.

Usually, the forms overlay is selected beforehand and is used successively so that t_{fo} is zero. The possibility that time might originally be required to locate the form raises an even larger question, namely, that of job setup time. It should be timed or estimated in minutes, divided by the estimated number of hours the job will run (including the job setup time), and the resultant subtracted from 60. Call it t_e. Then N_f should be multiplied by $t_e/60$ for a more realistic throughput estimate.

FILM FORMATS

For a discussion of optical reduction ratios, a review of Chapter 1 is appropriate. The most prevalent method of image recording at present is still single-frame or simplex (one-up) recording on roll film. As explained in Chapter 1, the image is compressed enough to permit two orientations. When one image is directly below its predecessor in a top-to-bottom sequence, the structure is like that of a motion picture film and the mode is therefore called "cine." On the other hand, a frame can be turned on its side so that the succession matches the side-by-side drawing of a comic strip. Because of this resemblance, this recording mode is called "comic." These formats are diagramed in Figure 3-12.

A less common structure also appears in Figure 3-12, namely, the two-up comic mode at 42X reduction. The obvious advantage of this technique is the utilization of lateral film area otherwise left blank and unused at the higher reduction factor. Longitudinally, of course, the increased reduction enables more frames to be fitted into the roll, but full advantage of this greater compression is realized only with double-frame recording. Recourse to a higher reduction factor naturally assumes that

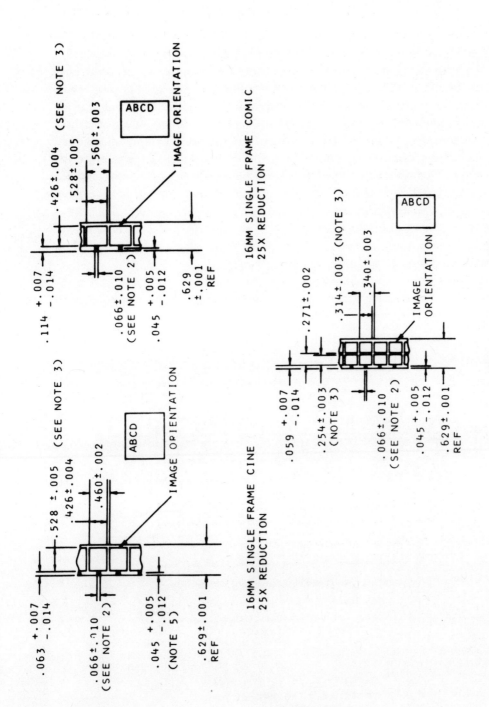

Fig. 3-12. Film formats of cine and comic frames.

41

the resolving power of the film as well as the optical system can preserve picture detail acceptably well. This condition is readily satisfied today.

Another problem implicit in double-frame recording doubtlessly explains why it is not more common. As examination of the illustration will confirm, the tolerances allowed for positioning the arrangement are rather stringent and the margin of permissible error is small. This situation creates a control problem with respect to camera-and-film movement that is especially burdensome with 16-mm film. It is more usual, therefore, to encounter two-up recording with 35-mm film. What is even more typical at present, and represents a strongly growing trend, is 8-up or 14-up recording on 105-mm film—in other words, microfiche formats. The objective is exactly the same as before, that is, to maximize film utilization and create a more useful form. The requirement of photo-optical control is greatly accentuated by the microfiche formats.

Figures 3-13 and 3-14 display the structures of 80-frame and 224-frame microfiche. The dimensions for the 80-frame fiche correspond to a reduction of 25X rather than 24X.

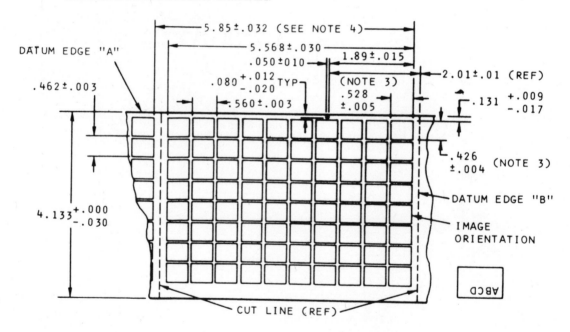

4 BY 6 (105 BY 148.75MM) FICHE
8 BY 10 = 80 FRAMES
25X REDUCTION

Fig. 3-13.   Typical COM microfiche at 25X reduction.

Referring once more to Figure 3-12, the solid blocks adjacent to the images along the edge of the film are sequential retrieval marks. These blips aid in the capture of a designated frame when a user subsequently wants to observe it on a reader screen.

In Figure 3-15, two-up and four-up recording on 35-mm film is shown. If the four-up format, especially, were cut into segments as 105-mm film is, another microfiche would be produced. This step, however, is not taken, and the film is transported through specially designed readers capable of displacing the image laterally for satisfactory viewing.

TITLING

Titling is the process of imprinting eye-readable characters, usually in two rows but sometimes only one, at the top of a microfiche for labeling purposes. Figure 1-2 is an example of titling that occupies only one row. (*Note:* The word "row" is used here to indicate that a user holding a microfiche would ordinarily turn it to make its longest dimension horizontal. The titling is placed along this dimension; when read, it seems to lie in a row. Since this edge lies along the length of the original 105-mm

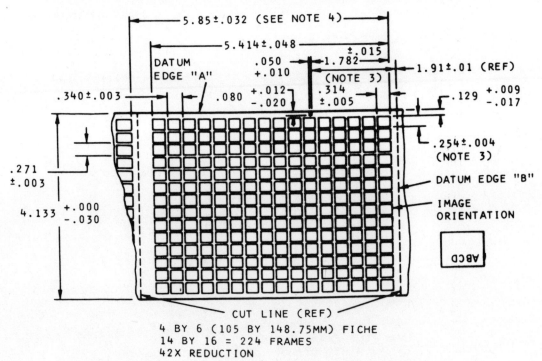

Fig. 3-14.   Typical COM microfiche at 42X reduction.

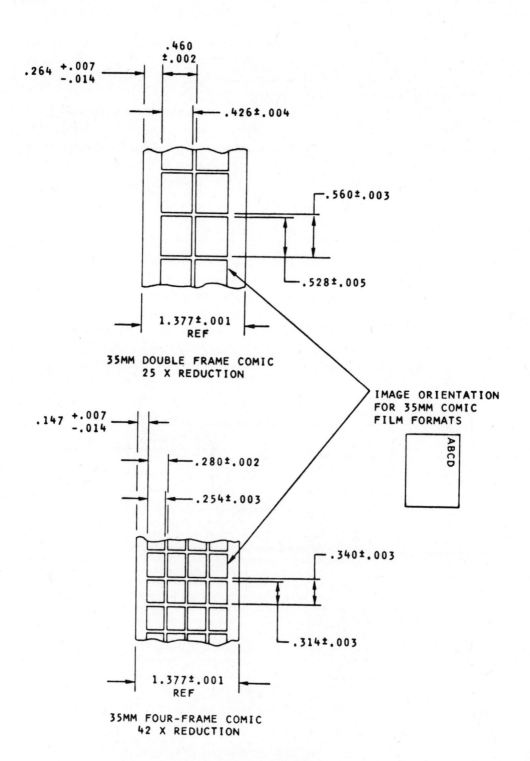

.460
±.002

.264 +.007
     -.014

.426±.004

.560±.003

.528±.005

1.377±.001
REF

35MM DOUBLE FRAME COMIC
25 X REDUCTION

IMAGE ORIENTATION
FOR 35MM COMIC
FILM FORMATS

ABCD

.147 +.007
     -.014

.280±.002

.254±.003

.340±.003

.314±.003

1.377±.001
REF

35MM FOUR-FRAME COMIC
42 X REDUCTION

Fig. 3-15.   Multiple-frame film formats.

film, however, the titling actually lies in a column, as far as the convention of recording is concerned.)

The great majority of COM recorders that perform titling today accomplish it with software programs or appropriate control signals on the source tape. In either case, some particular symbol like an "o," or an "x," or a bullet is repeatedly used to imprint closely spaced marks within a frame, and these small marks form characters to the unaided eye. The letters taken in succession across the row (or along the column with respect to the actual recording sequence) spell identifiable words. As mentioned, two lines of titles are usually printed.

An interesting hardware variation of this method has been introduced by the Terminal Data Corporation. Film is moved in front of an aperture plate that holds two columns of seven light-emitting diodes each (LED's). Only one of these two sets is activated at a time. In the active set, one or more diodes come on in each position of the film, which is then incremented to the next position. Since the character occupies five such spaces on the film, its formation obtains from a 5 x 7 matrix. Control over the photo-optical system requires much less computer space with this method than with the software method. Figure 3-16 shows how the characters are generated when using the aperture plate.

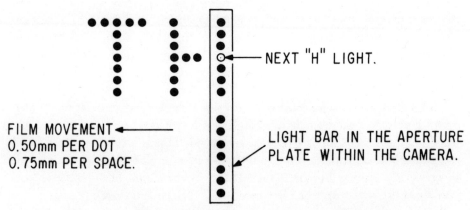

Fig. 3-16. Hardware titling method of Terminal Data Corp.

Once the form slide is drawn according to specifications and then converted into a film transparency, it can be projected onto the film in either of two ways. The usual method is illustrated in Figure 3-1. Note that the image is flashed onto a half-silver mirror by an intense strobe light, and enough light is reflected to the lens and onto the face side of the film to merge the format with the computer-generated data. This optical path is adjusted to reduce the slide to frame size on the film. The KOM microfilmers fall in this large category.

Another way is to project the form slide image on the reverse side of the film. This approach is illustrated in Figure 3-8, which, it will be recalled, represents the Memorex 1603 printer. Here the film passes between a dual lens system so that it receives an image from each lens, the alphanumerics on the front side and the application format on the rear side.

A consequence of the LED-imaging method of the 1603 printer is worthy of mention. As explained earlier, a line of alphanumerics is formed and recorded at a time, whereupon the film is incremented to the next character-line position. After the thirty-second line has been recorded, the form flash is ignited to record the form slide image. Evidently, it is only during this interval that the page-frame area of the film is in the proper position for the form slide image.

Still another form flash method is represented in Figure 3-10, which is a diagram of the Sequential s/COM-70. Here the form slide, or overlay, is of the same size as the diode image. Although it is not clear from the block diagram, the overlay is placed physically alongside the diodes so that its optical path through the lens onto the film will be identical with that of the diode image. The scale of the two images focused on the film will therefore be the same. Note that they are both recorded on the front side of the film. This technique has an interesting advantage. The tolerances put on the original form slide drawing, which in this case becomes the form overlay, can be relaxed somewhat since a certain discrepancy on a large drawing is less significant than the same error on a small drawing. The only critical requirement is that the flashing position of the slide be located accurately so that the two images will merge on the film as desired.

A final method of generating the application format is to store it in an internal control processor, from which it is recalled and drawn on the CRT screen at the same time the data is displayed. This is an extremely refined technique that is capable of creating complex engineering forms as well as relatively simple business formats. A microfilmer that employs this method is the well-respected Information International FR-80.

FORMS OVERLAY

In business and commercial computer applications a particular class of output data must often be imprinted on a specially designed format that is repeated throughout the data run. Naturally, it is convenient that this format, with its rows, its columns, and its headings, be superimposed upon the computer-generated data as part of the film image. In the COM industry this superposition is accomplished by several techniques.

The most common method of superposition employs a form slide. An example of such a slide appears in Figure 3-17. Used in both the Kodak KOM-80 and KOM-90 microfilmers, it is a 4 x 5-inch glass plate containing a photographic high-contrast image that is flash-projected onto the micro-

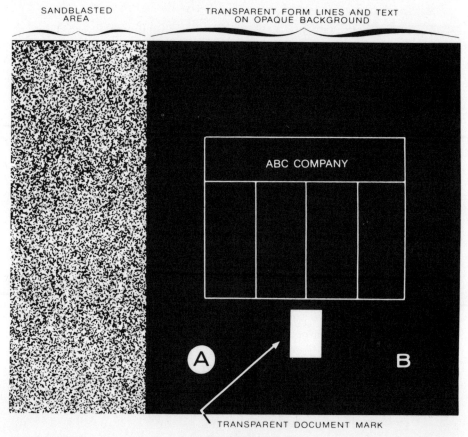

Fig. 3-17.   Form slide.

film. This information will be superimposed upon the data derived from the CRT—the computer-generated data, as mentioned previously. The edges of the glass plate are ground to assure accurate form location in the microfilmer. A translucent, sand-blasted area is provided for handling and identification purposes. Proper slide orientation is assured by means of photocells within the machine that sense two areas, specified as *A* and *B* in the figure. Area *A* must be clear and area *B* must be opaque. If these conditions are not met, the machine will stop when a form flash is signaled.

The form slide is photographed from a full-sixe (11 x 14 inches) art-work original supplied by the customer. It must specify the image orientation, the effective reduction ratio, and the form-to-text location.

COMPETING TECHNOLOGIES

The most serious competitor to COM is the device that has played the competitor's role all along—the impact printer. Competition is also offered by nonimpact printers, on-line computer systems with remote display terminals, conventional microfilmers, and precision plotters. For the reasons discussed previously, the extent of competition from any of these alternate output methods is not considered serious. For applications appropriate to its use, COM enjoys unique capabilities of controlling the mounting costs, weight, and volume of computer output while at the same time providing convenient data access and a permanent output record.

With respect to developments now in progress but not yet crystallized, it appears that photo-optical digital coding is about to surface as a completely new, perhaps even revolutionary, technology that may offer long-range competition to COM alphanumeric or graphic output.

Impact Line Printers

The arguments in favor of the impact line printer are just as valid now as they have been in the past. Its role will continue to be important when hard copy is required in many business applications and for shorter, more narrowly disseminated reports. The latter conditions are usually represented by output reports dealing with engineering or scientific calculations. Only a few individuals are generally concerned with the result, and an immediate permanent record is a convenience. The performance of impact printers is continually improving, as indicated by the recently announced IBM 3211 printer, which is rated at 2000 lines per minute.

Nonimpact Line Printers

For the relatively fast production of hard copy when duplicates are not required, the nonimpact line printer competes as much with the impact printer as it does with COM. Indeed, when COM is under consideration, the choice is not really between it and nonimpact printing but between microfilm and paper. Considered in this light, it is apparent that nonimpact printing acts as an obstacle to COM when it makes computer printouts more feasible or attractive. This situation is realized in data processing applications that employ nonimpact printers as auxiliaries to impact printers. Hence, if certain computer output has high priority, it is channeled to the nonimpact printer, or if graphic forms need to be constructed, they are executed by the nonimpact printer-plotter. This approach can make urgent data available sooner than when impact printers are not supplemented. It can also make an installation more interactive than an equivalent COM installation for which conventional film processing is used.

Obviously, an information manager who is satisfied with hybrid impact and nonimpact printing will be less receptive to the COM option and the transitional problems it imposes. In the lower-volume range of the market especially, the nonimpact printer may contribute to excluding computer output microfilm.

A number of reasonably priced nonimpact printers are available at the present time. Examples of the electrostatic principle are the Versatec Matrix printer-plotters, the Varian Associates Statos Models 5 and 21, the Info-Max 57 printer-plotter, and the Gould Model 4800 electrostatic printer-plotter.

The electrostatic technique has the advantage of no moving parts except those required to transport paper. A series of small electrodes, or nibs, is packed into a writing head that spans the printing width of the paper. A digital electronic raster scan determines which nibs on a particular line are activated, and the electrostatic stress these elements exert on the chemically treated paper produces tiny dark spots. As the paper is transported line by line, the dots are joined to form alphanumerics or graphic forms. Evidently, printing is synthesized by dot matrices, usually 5 x 7 in composition.

The Path System 1200 printer is classified as an electrographic rather than an electrostatic printer. In place of the dot-forming nibs, it employs a negative mask by which completely formed characters are projected onto plain bond paper. The mask, and therefore the font, can be changed by the operator. Paper rolls up to 2000 feet long can be installed; width of the paper should conform with the number of print positions. The manufacturer specifies a printing rate of 1200 lines per minute, regardless of line length.

Another nonimpact concept employs an electrostatically charged jet stream of ink that is deflected—much like an electron beam within a cathode-ray tube—before the droplets are deposited on a sheet of paper. The most adaptable ink-jet device is the A. B. Dick video jet printer, since it can be driven by virtually all the widely used computers as well as performing as a terminal. Its ink droplets are deflected by a video signal that is generated in response to the received character code. A 9 x 11 matrix forms the character. Another ink-jet printer, the Teletype Ink-

tronic printer, which is designed to serve only as a communications terminal, is not significant to the COM industry.

The Dick video jet printer executes about 100 lines per minute. The
Versatec printers achieve about 300 lines per minute. These are typical
rates, although more expensive devices can attain 800 and even 1000 lines
per minute. Since these rates are practically inert by COM standards, it
becomes even clearer that the nonimpact printer is influential in hindering
COM acceptance only in its capacity as a printing auxiliary, as previously
described.

Printer Output Microfilmer

An interesting alternative to the COM recorder is the printer output
microfilmer (POM). This equipment transfers a computer printout on continuous fanfold forms to microfilm. Once an exposed reel of film is obtained,
the same conditions that characterize a COM installation also apply to a
POM installation: The film has to be processed, it can be easily duplicated,
and it must be viewed in a reader. However, the speed advantage of the
COM recorder is sacrificed and the paper cost is not eliminated. For these
reasons, POM should have no more than a limited place in the market.

On-Line Display Terminals

For on-line applications, the computer output may be displayed directly on graphic display terminals when graphic forms are involved or
on alphanumeric display terminals when graphics are not required. Information is stored on magnetic tape or on a magnetic disk in digital form.
On-line display terminals are not expected to offer serious long-term
competition to COM recording because magnetic materials are more expensive than film and their storage density is lower by an order of magnitude.

Such on-line information storage and retrieval systems are thus more
expensive than the microfilm alternative, and this cost relationship will
continue. The added cost of an on-line computer application may be justified, however, when data base updating is required more frequently than
daily or when user interaction is required, as in an airline passenger reser-
vation system. Otherwise, COM will continue to compete favorably.

Precision Plotters

Precision digital plotters are an obvious but expensive alternative to
COM recorders. Moreover, their intended function is to generate the ex-

ceedingly precise line drawings that could previously be obtained only from a draftsman. Thus, the appropriate application of a precision plotter is less to display computer output than to execute a desired line drawing under the control of a properly programmed computer. Direct competition (favorable to COM) will result only if the precision graphics output of the higher-priced scientific recorders is of sufficient quality to serve this purpose.

FUTURE TRENDS

The direction of the COM industry in the next five years can in part be anticipated by the present state of the technology and level of research activity. Unfortunately, present economic conditions have slowed or disrupted the research and development devoted to COM so much that, except for possible laser applications, significant technological progress does not seem likely in the period through 1975.

Nevertheless, sufficient gains have been made in the past three years to enable further progress through the perfection of existing techniques and the refinement of product design. Further, part of the progress potential for COM lies in matching marketing skills to the existing product quality. For these reasons, the COM industry has adequate opportunity to move forward during the next five years.

Additionally, technological progress made in tangential areas may be more important to the future of COM than its own technology. If new procedures such as keyboard updating of photo-optical storage data were to come into vogue, or if there were a breakthrough in digitizing COM film in the OCR field, the impact on COM would be significant.

CIM and Film Memory

A breakthrough in the optical reading of microfilm would greatly benefit the COM industry because of the tremendous concentration of data contained in a unit measure of film. For example, at a reduction ratio of 24X, the equivalent of 2000 bits of information are compressed into a linear inch of film. By comparison, recording or magnetic tape can be effected at 800 bits per inch and 1600 bits per inch. (Certain aeronautical companies are said to be experimenting with 8000-bit-per-inch recording.) At a reduction ratio of 42X, the packing density increases to about 3500 bits per inch.

This linear measure, however, hardly reveals the true superiority of microfilm as a storage medium. To perceive its full power, one must consider packing density over an area and then make a comparison with the density of linear recording on tape or with the data recorded on a disk. In a report on computer microfilm published by Oppenheimer & Co., John K. Koeneman and John R. Schwanbeck state that over one million bits can be recorded on a square centimeter of microfilm, but only 1050 bits per square centimeter can be stored on magnetic materials. The figure given for microfilm is tantamount to 6,450,000 bits per square inch, and for magnetic materials, 6775 bits per square inch. Here, of course, the ratio of storage in the two mediums, namely, 1,000:1, is as important as the capacities.

We should recognize that the packing density on film varies in direct proportion to the reduction ratio employed. Unfortunately, Koeneman and Schwanbeck omitted mention of the reduction ratio on which their figures were based, doubtlessly because their intended audience had little interest in this parameter. Although the authenticity of the cited figures is not disputed, there is a desire to make the comparison between film and magnetics more definitive. For example, at a reduction ratio of 150:1—characteristic of some ultrafiche today—16,600,000 bits per square inch could be recorded. This figure, however, would not afford a fair comparison, since ultrafiche is not yet considered practical for COM.

At a reduction ratio of 24X, which today is prevalent, frame sizes tend to center on 0.55 x 0.55 inch. Since the standard computer printout format consists of 64 lines, each with 132 characters, informational content within the specified frame is normally equivalent to slightly less than 225,000 bits per square inch. At a reduction ratio of 42X, the density increases to about 685,000 bits per square inch. It is these figures, which better reflect actual recording techniques in vogue at present, that should be compared with the content on tape or on disks. Possibly, we should also postulate the case for which the vertical density is as great as that printed horizontally, that is, 132 x 132 characters in a frame. This stipulation, which represents what could readily be done with current methodology, leads to figures of 460,000 bits per square inch and 1,400,000 bits per square inch, respectively. Against a background of these figures, comparisons should be made with contents of 30 to 60 million bits on a reel of magnetic tape, 7.25 million bits on a 2311 type disk pack, 29 million bits on a 2316 type disk pack, and 100 million bits on a 3330 type disk pack.

Clearly, relatively small sections of film can hold substantially more information than the capacity of any of the previously mentioned magnetic devices. For this reason it is unfortunate that optical character reading is not a really practical technique for digitizing alphanumeric data on present computer output microfilm, and it is therefore not a prospective computer input microfilm, or CIM, exceptional situations aside. The loss is greater still when the permanence of a microfilm printout is considered, compared with the vulnerability of magnetic materials to both accidental and deliberate erasure. In view of the need for absolute reliability in transferring data from film to a computer, the solution of the CIM problem obviously lies in digital recording. The disadvantage of this approach, of course, is that the recorded data would not be eye-readable.

Digital Recording on Film

A number of companies, including IBM and Eastman Kodak, are presently developing systems for recording digitally on microfilm. The activity of IBM is particularly interesting in view of its indifference to COM. The company has, in fact, already delivered a trillion-bit storage system, utilizing the principle of spot recording, to the Atomic Energy Commission. This method simply darkens a tiny spot of film, 14 x 16 microns in size, or leaves a spot entirely clear. These minute dimensions permit recording 2½ million data bits per square inch. Taking into account error detection and correction codes mingled with the data to ensure accurate readout of the data bits, the aggregate packing density is slightly higher. Detection of the data bits, incidentally, has no need of elaborate technology like flying-spot scanners. A particularly useful property of the IBM system is its ability to produce any addressed data field within an average time of 3 seconds.

To inscribe a succession of opaque and clear spots, an electron beam first sweeps from left to right, alighting upon each area to be coded, where it oscillates back and forth over a tiny square if the area should be darkened, but cuts off if the area is to remain clear. On the next line the beam scans from right to left, and so on. The binary digit zero consists of a transparency followed by a spot; a 1 is a spot followed by a transparency. A trail of 1s introduces each track to calibrate the electronic detection circuits.

Diffraction-Grating Recording

A second method under development at the Kodak Research Labs is called diffraction-grating recording. Here a laser beam is split into two parts by a half-silver mirror. One component, called the reference beam, is deflected directly onto photographic film, while the second component, called the signal beam, is allowed to travel a greater distance before it is deflected back to the portion of film receiving the reference beam. This beam, entering the film directly, has a certain polarization structure, while the signal beam, impinging at an angle and having traveled a greater distance, has a distinctly different structure. As both penetrate the emulsified layer of the film, there are places where the phases reinforce and other places where the phases cancel. Naturally, the regions of energy reinforcement become dark bands on the film surface after processing. Since these bands are regular and evenly spaced, they are called diffraction-grating patterns. This analogy follows from the definition of a diffraction-grating, which is basically regarded as any periodic array of similar openings.

An opposing situation is created by suppressing the signal beam and admitting only the reference beam. Then the film emulsion is stimulated uniformly and no diffraction-grating pattern is formed. A binary condition has therefore arisen, since a 1 or a zero can be assigned according to whether a pattern is present or absent.

The properties of the diffraction pattern engraved on the film lead to an interesting readout process. When present, the grating will bend or diffract a laser beam passing through the film; when the pattern is absent, the beam will pass directly through. A photoemissive cell can be positioned to intercept emerging light in one situation or the other. Detection of the zeros and 1's is therefore a simple and reliable matter.

At this point, suppose a second signal beam is superimposed upon the reference beam. It, too, will cause the formation of a diffraction pattern, but the band spacing will differ from that of the original pattern. This effect is due to the difference in the phase relationships. Accordingly, light passing through the film will be bent at different angles by the two patterns. If two separate photodetectors are employed, each can determine whether its associated pattern is present or absent. Technology has so far been perfected to the point of permitting as many as 30 signal beams. Thus, in one recording space it is possible to embed 30 distinct data bits.

Two important characteristics of this recording method are now evident. First, each bit extends over a large area. The effect is to make detection easier and more reliable. Second, bits can be superimposed. This ability provides high packing densities, on the order of a half-million bits per square inch. A corollary advantage of large recording areas is that damage to them by dirt and scratches is proportionately less than to smaller areas. Another advantage of superimposed recording is that it enables parallel readout, often called simultaneous readout, with a corresponding increase in transfer rate. These attractive features of diffraction-grating augur many potential applications as computer memories.

Holographic Recording

A third method under extensive development, as reported at the 1971

National Convention of the Society of Photographic Scientists and Engineers, is holographic recording, frequently referred to as Fourier recording. This technology is really akin to diffraction recording in that the additive and canceling effect of reunited laser beams is utilized to produce on film a two-dimensional array of black and clear squares. Here, again, a binary situation exists. Not surprisingly, some of the advantages of diffraction recording are realized in holographic recording. The packing density tends to be somewhat lower than that yielded by other methods, but costs are quite low and detection is simple, reliable, and inexpensive. A distinguishing characteristic of holographic recording is that the recording medium is always held fixed during recording, whereas in the diffraction method, the recording medium may be in motion while recording is underway.

Information Storage and Retrieval

It is no exaggeration to assert that the most backward and disorganized function in American industry and commerce today is information storage and retrieval. Many documents are as good as lost forever because they cannot be retrieved when they are needed. Microfilm as a storage and retrieval medium is obviously appealing because of its economy, its information compression and concomitant space reduction, its convenience of handling, and the rapidity with which a COM recorder can reissue an updated computer file. Actually, it is more than merely appealing; microfilm should be considered a specific solution to the problem. Once the human factors barrier against converting to microfilm has worn away, COM will be more widely regarded as a fast and flexible way to generate film coded for systematic storage and fast retrieval.

Laser Technology and Impact

Laser technology holds the promise of ushering in a revolutionary generation of COM recorders. The significance of laser COM's is not their superspeed in the laboratory, where they are already writing five times faster than other recorders now marketed. At present this superior speed has limited application, since only the exceptional volume requirements of the largest insurance companies can fully utilize the printing rates already available. Of greater significance by far is the ability of laser beams to expose vesicular film (see Chapter 5) directly—its simple application of heat to the magazines develops the film and allows the COM recorder to deliver a completely processed film master. Thus, the annoyance and delays of external film processing, with its attendant plumbing and electric power problems, are eliminated.

To be sure, these advantages would have to be provided at relatively low cost, but laser technology has the inherent power to attain this goal. Certain corporations prominent for the negative reason of their absence from COM are said to be experimenting in this field. (Unfortunately, discretion precludes their identification.) It is predicted that laser technology will begin to unfold in the COM industry within two years.

4. CAMERAS AND THEIR ACTION
IN COM RECORDERS

INTRODUCTION

In contemplating the COM camera, one should really think in terms of a photo-optical system. Without belittling the accomplishment of a camera in reducing a real object to a compressed image on film, this action is but a small part of the overall series of functions—optical, mechanical, and electronic—that must be performed to produce a usable microfilm or microfiche. Hence, the camera is merely one component of a complex photo-optical system.

Recent advances in COM technology seem to have converged on the photo-optical section. One striking example discussed is LED-imaging technology. Other progress has consisted of diversifying the film-formatting capability of a single recorder to include fiche as well as microfilm. Still another important item has been the upgrading of system throughput by virtue of faster photo-optical action. In short, designers have finally turned their attention to the photo-optical system as a whole. They have redesigned the camera proper in accordance with its functions in the COM recorder; they have redesigned film-transport mechanisms and film-drive assemblies to perform with the speed required of COM components. Most important of all, perhaps, they have belatedly applied well-known principles of digital servocontrol to the particular demands of COM operation. Benefits of this multipronged attack on photo-optic design are beginning to be felt, and will be felt still more over the next two years.

Definition

Essentially, a photo-optical system consists of a lens assembly, the film-transport mechanism, the transport-drive assembly, the supply and take-up magazines, and the supply and take-up electric drive systems. An equally important portion of the system, but seldom an integral part of the camera unit, is the controller. It exerts precise control over the transport drive and coordinates all camera functions with other functions of the COM system. Options of the photo-optical system include image count mark, coding assemblies (Kodamatic,* Miracode,* etc.), and other specialties and film-condition indicators (footage remaining: 25 feet remaining; and out-of-film switches).

SYSTEM CAPABILITIES

As mentioned, advanced equipment today employs servosystems to transport film and move mechanical assemblies in the film-recording process. Many systems, however, still use stepper motors. Early microfilmers relied on clutch-brake mechanisms in combination with dc motors.

Indeed, until quite recently, the camera was regarded simply as a noncritical component of the overall complex. The most suitable off-the-shelf cameras were selected and adapted to operate with other system components. Typically, they had been developed for aircraft flight instrumentation recording and were not required to advance film rapidly, run at high film rates, run thousands and thousands of feet without service, or be operated by nontechnical personnel.

Even today the imperfect mechanical performance of surprisingly many COM cameras leads to operational delays and other problems. These are quite minor, however, compared with the inadequacies of the cameras originally adapted. These models suffered from an abundance of ills, and film scratching, skewing, pinching, snagging, and jamming were frequent. Occasionally outright breakage also occurred. A particularly serious shortcoming of the early improvisations was their inexact and sometimes erratic frame registration. For precision work, sprocketed film was a virtual necessity. Another drawback of photo-optical systems not especially designed to meet COM needs is sluggish operation, which diminishes system throughput. Even today this condition is far too prevalent.

The basic action still standard in most roll-film recorders today con-

---

*Kodamatic and Miracode systems are registered trademarks of Eastman Kodak Company.

sists of the following sequence: light from images formed on a CRT screen passes through a half-silver mirror to a camera; when the entire image has been completed, a transparent forms overlay is flashed by a strobe light to the mirror and reflected to the camera in superposition with the CRT image; and the composite image is focused by a lens on the film. A motor then advances the film to the next recording position. Such cameras print a series of single frames along the film length in either cine (top edge to bottom) or comic (left edge to right) mode.

In order to imprint frames across the film width, whether in a two-up format on 16- or 35-mm film or across any rows of 4 x 6-inch fiche (105-mm film), the step-and-repeat action of a universal camera is needed. One technique causes the lens to move along the film in discrete steps, row by row, until the last frame is recorded, whereupon the camera returns to its starting position and a motor precisely increments the film into position for the next column. DatagraphiX and Wollensak employ this method. System logic generating commands in response to the controlling program governs the entire sequence. This procedure is called "vertical pagination."

TYPES OF CAMERAS

Nonperforated (Strip) Camera

The 16-mm strip camera records images on nonperforated film, either for readers with manual film transport or for readers with automatic random-access capabilities. The specified image is situated on the display screen by visually sighting it and adjusting the film position manually, or by automatically stopping at an image count or frame mark recorded on the film adjacent to the image frame. Unless the code mark is recorded in its proper position, frame recapture will not be accurate. Nevertheless, the positioning of the image on the film relative to adjacent images, usually referred to as frame registration, is not considered critical. Generally, tolerances of ±0.002 to ±0.005 inch are quite acceptable. The image-to-film-edge tolerance is normally ±0.001 to 0.002 inch, owing to the capability of the reader to present the image on the screen with sufficient latitude to accept the tolerance.

High-Resolution/Graphic Arts Camera

Graphic systems require the ability to butt frames quite accurately so that successive drawings can be presented continuously. This requires a frame registration accuracy to within ±0.001 inch, and is often required to be within ±0.0005 inch.

The greater accuracy has been realized so far only by using perforated film and registration pins. Thus, one predetermined pulldown distance, film size, and perforation type (such as Kodak standard or Bell and Howell) are possible for each camera. These transports are quite expensive. Multiple-format applications would require several cameras.

Microfiche Camera

Aside from the advantages and disadvantages of microfiche, the microfiche camera represents a severe problem to the camera designer. Unfortunately, users need a camera to execute all formats, carry out all filming sequences, and possibly provide all fiche sizes with various concepts of titling. Furthermore, the camera must fit into the cabinet space that holds the 16-mm camera, and its cost cannot exceed that of the 16-mm size.

A practical fiche camera is a complex compromise. Although 105-mm film is heavy and hard to handle, it must be moved quickly and with great precision. The film has to move through the aperture bidirectionally to generate the rows, and something else has to move across the film to create the columns. There are three methods to accomplish the latter:

1. Move the whole film transport across the lens field.

2. Move the film transport across the lens, but retain the film supply and take-up in a fixed position.

3. Maintain the film platen and supply take-up fixed, and move the optics across the film.

A fiche camera has many variables to consider in generating a fiche. The variables are as follows:

Column margin	Number of pages per fiche recorded
Row margin	Number of fiche recorded per run
Column page increment	Sequence of operation
Row page increment	Initial starting point of sequence
Column number of pages	Page-advance command
Row number of pages	Fiche-advance command
Title position	Page-advance complete
Number of rows per titling	Fiche-advance complete
Number of columns per titling	Low-film indication
Orientation on film of titling	Out-of-film indication
Fiche length	Cut-mark application

The requirements for a microfiche camera obviously are much more complex than those for the 16-mm camera. As a result, the control electronics alone is more complex than that of the complete two-axis servo-drive system.

The Wollensak 303, shown in Figure 4-1, is an example of a microfiche camera.

Fig. 4-1.   Wollensak Model 303, a microfiche camera.
(Courtesy of Wollensak, Inc.)

FILM TRANSPORT MECHANISMS

The nonperforated film must be moved rapidly, precisely, and without slippage. Essentially, there are only two ways of driving nonperforated film continuously (see Figure 4-2): pinch roller drive and capstan drive. Both concepts have merits and drawbacks.

The pinch roller relies on squeezing the film between a driving roller and a free-floating, spring-loaded roller. The pressure of the spring-loaded

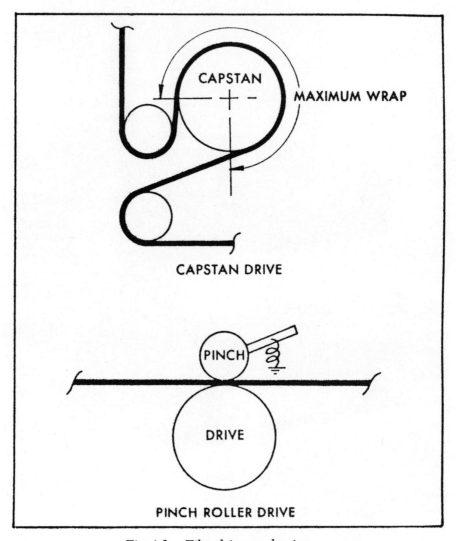

Fig. 4-2.   Film-drive mechanisms.

roller on the film to the drive wheel reduces the probability of film slippage, but the contact is really line contact. Therefore, rapid acceleration of this drive wheel can spin the wheel against the film and create static electricity, which may result in film slippage and poor frame registration. On the other hand, the pinch roller does not require high film tension on the supply and take-up side to retain the drive friction. The price paid is to permit the camera to continue to drive film, with a take-up failure resulting in a film jam. The limiting factor of this system also is associated with how firmly the film can be pinched without actually exposing the film at the line of contact.

The capstan drive, when properly designed, eliminates slippage of the film by not creating static electricity. The film must be wrapped around the capstan as much as possible and the film tension must be relatively high. This provision also greatly reduces the probability of a jam as the capstan stops driving the film when tension is lost.

A major problem in the use of COM is that of running through a complete print cycle only to discover that the camera has jammed so that no images have been produced. A well-designed capstan system can avert this situation, since it must have both supply and take-up film tension to operate. Since the mechanism cannot drive without these forces, the film is released if it breaks or if the take-up fails to hold. The system can be shut down in this eventuality. In addition, the film cannot bunch up between the capstan and the take-up magazine because the capstan film movement also relies on the take-up film tension. Without it the film will not move, and without movement the bunching cannot occur. Another benefit of continuous tension is that there is no snapping action; no free loops to get pulled tight, to snap, or to bunch up; and no secondary pinch rollers to move the film in and out of the transport. This kind of movement would generate more electricity, breakage, and jamming.

Drive Considerations

The drive mechanism must accelerate from zero to a specific angular velocity and decelerate to a complete stop in such a way that the film is not subjected to undue stress; nor can these decelerations be of such magnitude that the film slips or induces compliance in the film-drive material.

There are many different methods of driving rotating objects electrically and through other modes of power. However, the requirements for small size, low inertia, high speed, and light weight preclude most of them. The rate of acceleration and deceleration plus the high velocities required to achieve the necessary pulldowns also eliminate such items as standard dc motors; stepper motors are undesirable as well. The latter can be utilized to a certain extent, but complex ramping-speed control and other means have to be utilized. Even with all this trickery, steppers have the characteristics of multiple-step functions, with the associated high step-function acceleration, marginal positional accuracies, and inherent probability of losing a step.

BENEFITS OF IMPROVED CAMERA AND PHOTO-OPTICAL DESIGN

The various benefits of adept photo-optical design previously mentioned, and others that can be realized through further design refinement, are summarized below.

The new recording formats—such as 224-frame microfiche recorded on 105-mm film at a reduction ratio of 42X, two-up imaging on 16-mm film, and four-up imaging on 35-mm film—have become practicable only because of tremendous improvement in the precision of electronic and servo-control of the photo-optical components. These concentrated formats all demand tight butting of frames, and the tolerances for their location within the recording area are far more stringent than those that could be implemented only a few years ago. High-density recording means, of course, that film is being used more economically than previously. Any procedure that appreciably lowers the aggregate cost of a frame of printed output makes a COM system more salable to that extent.

Even denser microfiche formats might be anticipated as the electro-mechanical precision of optical-component movement improves further. Such formats, however, may be delayed by limitations in system resolving power. One instance is film. Would the cost of film capable of preserving detail at a reduction of, say, 55X be modest enough to preserve the economies inherent in such recording? A second consideration is image blowback. Would the readers provide adequate resolution and trouble-free operation at a low enough price to sustain the economies of recording at still higher reduction ratios? Both questions should be answered affirmatively before this kind of recording is introduced.

The reduction of much detrimental action such as skewing and jamming of film has greatly improved the attitude of users in the past two years. Further improvement, especially in the 42X reduction mode, would help still more.

The photo-optical section should cost less. In one sophisticated COM system that costs about $90,000, the photo-optical section can execute multiformats on any type of film, but unfortunately at a price of about $28,000. At present this figure is really not unreasonable in light of what the instrument can do. Nevertheless, it represents a huge potential for savings if new technological strides can make the same functions available at less cost.

The mechanism must index film still faster. Recently, frame pulldown times on the order of 10 msec have been appearing, and the boost in throughput that results from this characteristic alone is shown in the examples given below. What is needed now is equally short index times in microfiche execution (time to move either the film or lens from one frame to the next adjacent frame) and corresponding reductions in the traverse time (time required to return to the starting point of a succeeding column after recording the last frame in the column being formed). Another and perhaps a wiser way of using the resultant improvement in system performance is to trade it for a lower product price by substituting cheaper electronic components that keep throughput at its original level.

Example 1

Suppose a microfilmer prints at the rate of 60 Kc/sec and the film pulldown time for indexing to the next frame position is 100 msec. The time required to write a standard computer printout, which consists of 64 lines of 132 characters per line, is 141 msec. The execution time from the top of one frame to the next is therefore 241 msec. Hence, the throughput will be 249 pages per minute (ignoring all other time delays).

Now suppose the pulldown time is reduced to 10 msec. If no other change is made, the same machine will now produce 398 pages per minute. If the machine is redesigned with cheaper components to produce the same page count as before, it will need to write at the reduced rate of 37 Kc/sec.

Example 2

Suppose the machine again prints at the rate of 60 Kc/sec but has a pulldown time of 40 msec. The throughput of this combination would be 332 pages per minute.

Again let us suppose that the pulldown time is reduced to 10 msec. Once more the same machine will produce 398 pages per minute. If the machine were redesigned to maintain the original throughput of 332 pages per minute, it would have to write at the rate of 60 Kc/sec.

Both examples show that remarkable improvements in system performance can be realized through the introduction of a 10-msec pulldown time. The examples also show that if the unproductive intervals consumed in film indexing are shortened, the cost of a COM system designed to achieve a specified standard of operation can be commensurately reduced.

Table 4-1. Manufacturers of COM Cameras

MANUFACTURER OR DISTRIBUTOR	MODEL	FILM OUTPUT	REMARKS
Canon U.S.A., Inc. (distributor)	Various pulse-data cameras	Consult mfr.	Japanese manufacturer says that various existing cameras are adaptable to COM recording
Vought Division of Computer Equipment Corp.	Microfiche data recorder (VDR-MF1)	105 mm only	Separate lens for each reduction ratio (24X, 42X); controller set up for each format; perf. film movement
	Microfiche data recorder (VDR-MF1s1)	16 and 105 mm, interchangeable	Separate lens for each reduction ratio (24X, 42X); controller set up for each film format; perf. film movement
	Microfiche data recorder	35 and 105 mm, interchangeable	Separate lens for each specified reduction ratio; controller set up for each film format; double perf. film movement
	Microfilm data recorder	16-mm nonperf. only	Vought cameras installed in 80-85% of current COM installations
Cubic Corp.	FT-700	16 mm	Model consists of film transport only based on magnetic-tape movements; no optics
Memorex Corp.	1603 photo-optical system	16 mm	Not a camera in the conventional sense; see Chapter 3
Pacific Optical Company (division of Bourns, Inc.)	LR 16/35	16, 35 mm	Film size set by small adjustment in camera body; uses one set of magazines and adapter plates; film-footage meters mounted on magazine; company specifies frame accuracies to within ±0.002" for 2.031" film pulldown; frame advances in multiples of 0.0098" can be programmed by main frame or set by camera controller.
SEACO Computer Display, Inc.	Microfiche recorder	105 mm	Rights to microfiche camera developed by Image Sciences, Inc., and Walter Renold acquired by SEACO Computer Display, Inc., which will manufacture and market the camera to the micrographics industry as well as using it in its COM recorders. Camera should be available by end of November 1971 after completion of modifications by SEACO.

Company	Camera	Film format	Description
Sequential Information Systems, Inc.	Microfilm camera s/COM-70	16 mm nonperf.	Designed for s/COM-70 LED imaging technique
	Universal camera s/COM-70	16 and 105 mm, interchangeable	Separate lens and controller setup for each film format
Stromberg-DatagraphiX, Inc.	F 230 Universal camera	16 and 105 mm, interchangeable	Now installed as standard equipment in all DatagraphiX business COM recorders; DatagraphiX 4060 retains standard Vought camera (either 16 or 35 mm)
Terminal Data Corp.	DisplayMate DMF-2	16, 35, 70, 82.5, and 105 mm	Designed expressly for COM recorders employing cathode-ray tubes but lacking an internal processor; capable of reduction ratios from 10 to 50X
	DisplayMate DMF-3	16, 35, 70, 82.5, and 105 mm	Designed expressly for COM recorders employing cathode-ray tubes and having an internal processor; capable of reduction ratios from 10 to 50X
	DisplayMate DMF-4	16, 35, 70, 82.5, and 105 mm	Designed for COM recorders that do not use a CRT display; reduction ratios from 10 to 50X
	VERSAFORM	16, 35, 70, 82.5, and 105 mm	A DMF-2 modified by both Terminal Data and Eastman-Kodak for use in Kodak KOM-80 and KOM-90 microfilmers
Wollensak, Inc.	302 and 304 COM cameras	16 mm nonperf.	Models differ only in physical orientation of magazines and mounting; fast film pulldown (about 10 msec)
	303 Microfiche camera	105 mm	All main microfiche formats; fast page advance (20-40 msec)
	305 Universal COM camera	16, 35, 105 mm, interchangeable	Superseded by 306, with which it is similar except for use of sprockets
	306 Universal COM camera	16, 35, 105 mm, interchangeable	Utilizes perforated or nonperforated film; does not need registration pins or sprockets

DESCRIPTION OF EQUIPMENT

Table 4-1 is a list of the manufacturers that presently market COM camera systems and shows the models they offer. The following discussion describes many salient characteristics of some of the more advanced equipment now available.

DatagraphiX Universal Camera

The DatagraphiX F230 Universal camera (see Fig. 4-3) records images on 16-mm or 105-mm film in any of several formats. Cameras used in different equipment are functionally identical and differ only in interface logic.

The camera operates at a maximum speed of from 4.4 to 5.1 full data

Fig. 4-3.   DatagraphiX Universal camera used in DatagraphiX 4360 and 4440 Micromation printers. (Courtesy of Stromberg-DatagraphiX, Inc.)

frames per second, depending upon the format selected and the printing rate of the system. It has no shutter, since the exposure time of each character in a frame is controlled by the unblanking time of the display.

The Universal camera combines film movement with lens movement to provide a variety of film formats. Since film format is determined by the selected positions of the Universal camera control-panel switches, the programmer must provide switch-setting information to the operator along with the usual job instructions. The lens is moved across the film in discrete steps to form a column, and the film is advanced in discrete steps to form a row.

Three modes of lens movement are available for microfiche formats, with the lens movement always starting from the reference edge of the film. The reference edge is on the same side as the cut mark. In the zigzag mode, the lens steps along one column and back the next, recording in alternately opposite directions. In the slew-left mode, the lens steps (recording) along one column, and then slews back to the beginning position to start recording the next column. In the slew-right mode, the lens slews out before starting to record, steps (recording) back to the beginning position, and then slews out again to start recording the next column. These recording modes are illustrated in Figure 4-4.

ZIGZAG
SEQUENCE   SLEW RIGHT   SLEW LEFT

LENS MOVEMENT MAY BE SUMMARIZED BY SAYING THAT THE RECORDING SEQUENCE IS TOP TO BOTTOM, BOTTOM TO TOP, OR TOP TO BOTTOM TO TOP TO BOTTOM (ZIGZAG) OF A MICROFICHE.

Fig. 4-4.   Slewing modes of DatagraphiX Universal camera.
(From *AUERBACH Graphic Processing Reports.*)

The camera is equipped with interchangeable lens assemblies identified as 25X and 42X. The 25X indicates that the printed image on the film must be enlarged 25 times for full-size viewing or for printing hard copy. The 42X indicates that the image must be enlarged 42 times. The size of the film image when using the 42X lens (0.254 x 0.314 inch) is slightly more than one-half the size of the film image when using the 25X lens (0.426 x 0.528 inch). With the 25X lens, 16-mm film is printed with a single frame occupying most of the lateral width of the film (one-up). With the 42X lens, two images can be printed side by side (two-up) by moving the lens across the 16-mm film.

Magnetic tape or computer programs formatted for a DatagraphiX Micromation printer with a standard camera produce microfiche in the Universal camera without reformatting. The film format is determined

Fig. 4-5.   Vought 16-mm strip camera, nonperforated only. (Courtesy of Computer Equipment Corp., Vought Division.)

by the Universal camera-control switches. When a microfiche is filled, the film is automatically advanced to the next microfiche; each microfiche contains the same number of frames.

Producing film on which some or all microfiche are partially filled requires specially formatted input. The final frame advance of a partially filled microfiche is programmed by an AW or FW action code (fiche advance). Each microfiche in a series must be of the same physical size; therefore, the Universal camera steps the film through the remaining col-

Fig. 4-6.   Vought Universal camera with 35-mm double perforation movement. (Courtesy of Computer Equipment Corp., Vought Division.)

umn(s) in the partially filled microfiche and advances to the next microfiche.

Software-generated microfiche titling is accomplished by programming an x action code (titling mode) as the first character of a frame. In
titling mode, all subsequent x's within the print records of the frame cause
parity symbols ( ) to be printed. The x's are programmed to generate parity
symbols in proper position so that they build up a single large character
in the frame. Typically, the title characters are placed at the edge along
the length of the microfiche, although they may be placed in any frame
of the microfiche. Titling along the length of a partially filled microfiche
is accomplished by an AX action code (column advance). The column advance enables completing the title without the necessity of inserting a
series of dummy frame advances.

Vought Cameras

At present there are three main cameras marketed by the Vought
Division of the Computer Equipment Corporation, and they all comprise
the backbone of the COM industry in terms of actual installations. Not
long ago, Vought's share of installed equipment was as high as 90 percent.
Not surprisingly, this dominance is yielding some ground in face of the
onslaught of new competition, but the persistence of Vought cameras in
the field implies reliability of operation and other worthwhile attributes
that command respect.

Vought's 16-mm strip camera appears in Figure 4-5. Figure 4-6 displays its Universal camera with a 35-mm double-perforation movement.
Finally, Figure 4-7 displays its Universal camera with a 16-mm double-
perforation movement.

In the discussion that follows, general features of the Vought line are
explained.

Vought cameras are designed to record the output of a cathode-ray
tube on microfilm. The company does not yet have an instrument to record LED-generated images.

All Vought recorders have the following in common: mounting pattern; distance from mount to optical center, in both axes; distance from
mounting pattern to film plane. The electronic systems differ slightly, but
they are basically similar.

Cameras utilizing nonperforated film may be provided with pulldown
and aperture specifications that comply with the customer's requirements. Units with pulldown varying from 0.020 to 2.06 inches are in production. In the case of perforated film, pulldown normally depends on the
sprocket holes. Nevertheless, an accommodation for specific tasks can still
be made.

Pulldown and settling times vary, depending on the unit. Combined pulldown and settling times as low as 30 msec have been achieved; the average time is 40 msec.

These cameras are driven by three motors. A d-c 28-volt stepper motor provides the basic film-indexing capability, and two synchronous motors control supply and take-up film action by means of loop sensing.

Fig. 4-7.   Vought Universal camera with 16-mm double perforation movement. (Courtesy of Computer Equipment Corp., Vought Division.)

Various retrieval marks and codes can be provided on film. The following list is representative of the kinds available.

Retrieval Marks	*Retrieval Codes*
Void	Miracode (14 bar)
Timing	Kodamatic (21 bar)
Image count	Kodamatic (26 bar)
Frame count	

Accuracy of pulldown depends on the presence or absence of perforations, pulldown increment, reduction ratio, and so on. Frame-to-frame accuracies of ±0.0015 inch have been provided for butting requirements in both 16- and 35-mm nonperforated films.

Vought cameras require the following types of power: a-c 115 volt; d-c 28-volt pulse with switching capability for four sets of motor windings. Details on the pulse requirements are provided upon receipt of specific requirements.

Magazines are the split type and are interchangeable for use in either the supply or take-up position. The magazines provide a visual readout of film footage and provide a low film signal when 10 feet of film remains. Magazines are available in the capacities shown in Table 4-2.

Table 4-2. Magazine Capacities

FILM SIZE, MM	CAPACITY, FEET
16	400
16	600
16	1000
35	400
35	600

Boresight tools for focusing and alignment have been designed for all models. Magnifications available for this process are 10X or 20X.

Terminal Data DisplayMate Cameras

The Terminal Data Model DMF-2 (see Fig. 4-8) is designed to make high-quality microfiche and microfilm recordings of alphanumeric or plotted data displayed on cathode-ray tubes. It is intended for systems that do not have an internal processor.

This camera is capable of interchangeably recording in both fiche and linear format. The associated control system (see Fig. 4-9) provides inputs

Fig. 4-8.　Terminal Data DisplayMate DMF-2 multiformat recorder.
(Courtesy of Terminal Data Corp.)

and outputs for automatic operation directly from computers and controls normally associated with cathode-ray tube information systems.

Changes in fiche format or fiche-to-linear transfers are effected by simple changes in the camera and controls. Easily removable and replaceable magazines with either 100- or 400-foot capacity are available. The 100-foot magazine is made for 105-mm (4.133-inch), 3¼-inch, or 3-inch microfilm. A model of this magazine will permit the removal of short lengths of film after exposure. This feature provides rapid access to small amounts of data without waiting until an entire roll of film is used and then having to rethread the camera or take-up magazine. The 400-foot is made for 35-mm microfilm (unperforated) and 16-mm microfilm (unperforated).

A series of interchangeable lenses is available for different magnifications and different formats, all of which will provide high resolution and speed. The entire front carrying the indexing assembly is field removable and replaceable; therefore, other assemblies for unusual film formats can be readily installed.

Control and power circuitry are packaged in a separate unit, which is connected to the camera with a plug and cable. Integrated circuits are used almost exclusively for logic and control.

Terminal Data claims that throughput is enhanced by its unique design of film indexing and pulldown mechanisms. This claim is based on the pull-down time of 40 msec, which is a respectable increment, and precision in both design and manufacture of the camera. The company also states that this precision results in unusual and reproducible accuracy in microfiche imaging, regardless of format.

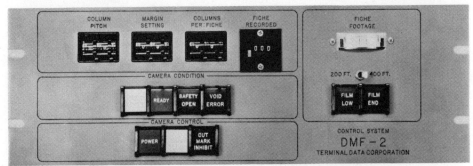

Fig. 4-9.   Front panel of DMF-2 control system. (Courtesy of
Terminal Data Corp.)

The Terminal Data Model DMF-3 is a digitally controlled microfilm camera designed for use in COM systems that contain an internal processor. It produces high-quality microfilm recordings of alphanumeric and/or plotted data presented on cathode-ray tubes in linear and/or microfiche formats using 16-mm, 35-mm, 70-mm, 82.5-mm, and 105-mm roll microfilm. The DMF-3 camera is capable of recording in interchangeable formats in both the linear and microfiche modes of operation.

The manufacturer believes that this camera benefits the user because it:

1. reduces operating costs that result from higher throughput rates.

2. increases packing (information) density of the microfiche formats compared with linear formatting.

3. permits the DMF-3 to fit into existing COM installations.

4. is an exceptionally simple and reliable system operating at high speed with maximum microimage resolution.

5. allows direct utilization of control codes from the host computer or the COM magnetic tape controller so that automatic operation is effected.

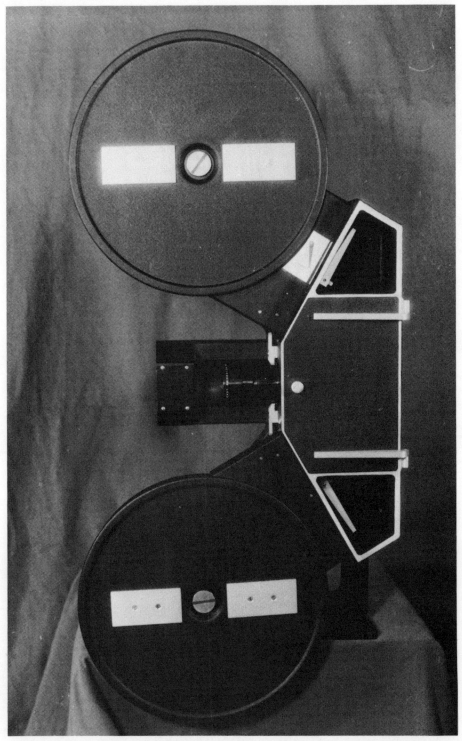

Fig. 4-10.   Wollensak Model 302 camera. (Courtesy of Wollensak, Inc.)

Terminal Data also claims that operational reliability is outstanding. The camera is a conservatively designed, economical system with built-in ruggedness and longevity. Maintenance is facilitated by the accessibility of all parts. No special tools are required to remove, replace, or service any of the system subassemblies.

Wollensak High-Speed Cameras

The Wollensak Models 302 and 304 COM cameras are identical except in the physical orientation of the magazines and mounting. The Model 302 permits maximum CRT-to-film-plane distance for a given cabinet space. A direct mechanical interchange of the Model 304 can be made with several other cameras currently on the market.

Models 302 and 304, shown in Figures 4-10 and 4-11, utilize a specially developed camera-drive system that advances 16-mm nonperforated film rapidly and precisely; for example, 0.376 inch is moved in 8 msec, 0.5 inch in 10 msec, and 0.65 inch in 12 msec. These figures include film settling as well as the actual advance time. These short pulldown times enable the camera to operate at frame rates of at least 100 frames per second. To determine the maximum frame rate corresponding to a pulldown time, allow approximately 1 to 2 msec in addition to the foregoing pulldown/settling times. For example: the 0.376-inch pulldown time is 8 msec; therefore assume a 10-msec frame-rate period. This is equivalent to 100 frames per second.

The positional accuracy of the standard 302 or 304 models is ±0.002 inch, nonaccumulative. This figure can be further improved with the introduction of a feedback control system. The control system is designed to provide the COM user with maximum flexibility via one selector switch. Seven different positions select "preset" page-advance distances in multiples of 0.002 inch. In addition, the controller will advance the camera 0.10 inch per pulse when a secondary signal is received for multiple Miracode columns.

The 303 fiche camera, shown in Figure 4-1, utilizes a unique design concept (patents pending) that eliminates reliance on friction to move the film. There are no pinch rollers to skew the film, no capstans to slip and cause positional errors, and no cumbersome leaky vacuum capstans to break down and interrupt system operation. The drive utilizes the same basic high-response servosystems used in the 16-mm cameras to position the film bidirectionally. As a result, a fiche up to 8 inches long can be randomly exposed without moving either the supply or take-up portions

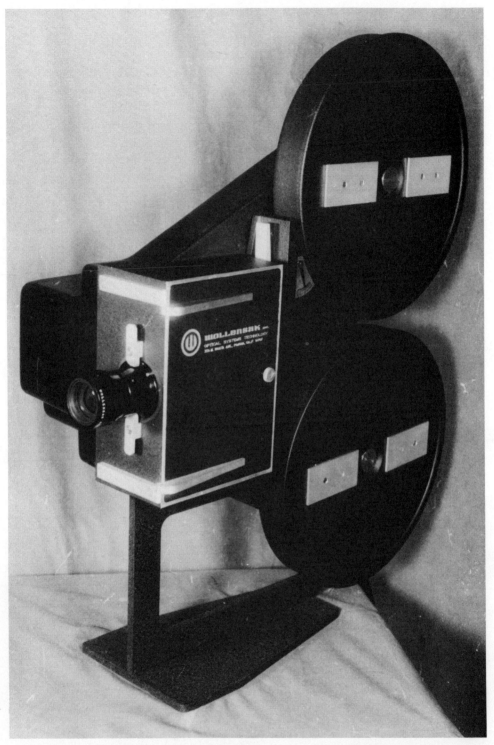

Fig. 4-11. Wollensak Model 304 camera. (Courtesy of Wollensak, Inc.)

79

of the film. The transverse positioning of the images is carried out by trans-porting the lens with a similar servosystem.

The two drives will normally position ½-inch increments in 40 msec (index time), with full 8-inch retrace accomplished in less than 100 msec, including settling (traverse time).

The 303 camera system consists of three basic components: camera mechanism, camera controller, and camera programmer. The manufacturer states that the combination of the 303 camera mechanism and controller produces an exceptionally fast, versatile fiche camera. Both zigzagging and titling are available.

Wollensak offers its new Model 306 COM camera as a replacement for the standard Universal camera and the six transports required with one camera and one integral transport. At the same time the new camera is said to provide more controllability, throughput, and accuracy than are afforded by existing Universal cameras. The following capabilities are claimed:

1. Perforated or nonperforated film can be used without equipment alteration.

2. A change from 16-mm to 35-mm film, or vice versa, can be made by changing apertures.

3. Advance distances are preset or remotely programmed.

4. Advance increments are finite and variable.

5. Frame-to-frame positioning is within ±0.0005 inch.

6. Frame-to-perforation alignment is made without registration pins or sprockets.

7. Cumulative error is zero with perforated film.

SEQUENTIAL INFORMATION SYSTEMS

The action of the Sequential photo-optical system is described in Chapter 3 in connection with LED imaging. Since the company claims that its film transport mechanism can index linearly recorded film at the rate of 1 msec per character line of film displacement, there may be an interest in utilizing Sequential motors and control components in present installa-tions and with existing cameras. For the sake of completeness, therefore, attention is drawn to the offer of this company to provide its components on an OEM basis.

5. FILM PREPARATION AND USE

INTRODUCTION

The type of film exposed in the recording operation of the COM system itself is invariably a silver halide. Visible light emanating from a cathode-ray tube is the usual source, but in LED imaging, infrared and sometimes visible red energy, depending on the emissive properties of the selected diodes, is employed instead. Film sensitive to only this narrow band of radiation is less expensive than conventional types. Another exception is film prepared for the 3M EBR recorder, which reacts to the energy relinquished by the impacting electron beam and is then processed by exposure to heat in an internally contained chamber.

Characteristics of Films

Silver halide films have many desirable characteristics that account for their widespread acceptance. First, they offer a high degree of resolution, with 100 to 160 lines per millimeter a practical COM standard, and 190 lines per millimeter a practical upper limit. Although higher resolutions have been claimed for both diazo and vesicular film under laboratory conditions, certainly silver halide film can achieve the finest detail of any film responsive to ordinary light sources and probably of any film type performing in an application environment. As we shall now see, however, this statement does not necessarily hold for film used in microfilmers. Indeed, a particularly stringent condition is imposed on master film used in COM recorders to

81

photograph the computer output, whether displayed on a CRT screen or by an LED array.

Film used in the COM system must be extremely fast acting in order to capture the image within the transitory period of its persistence. This requirement bars the highest grades of film from consideration because they are too slow. Faster reaction is accomplished at the cost of a somewhat grainy structure and moderately reduced resolution compared with the disqualified film grades. Accordingly, the figure of roughly 160 lines per millimeter was previously given as the resolution limit of COM film. Micromation microfilm®* (MMF), which Stromberg-DatagraphiX employs in its machines, is rated at 155 lines per millimeter.

---

*The name Micromation microfilm is a registered trade name of Stromberg-DatagraphiX, Inc.

Table 5-1.   Basic Duplication Costs of Film

		COST PER FILM DUPLICATE, CENTS*			
(A)		(B)	(C)	(D)	(E)
FILM USED AND ASSUMED NUMBER OF IMAGES PER 100 FEET OF FILM		LIMITED RUN, OUT-OF-HOUSE	LARGE-SCALE RUN, OUT-OF-HOUSE	STANDARD FILM OUT-OF-HOUSE	LOWER FILM GRADE IN-HOUSE
16 mm					
(24X)	1,800	0.277	0.203	0.167	0.107
	2,000	0.250	0.183	0.150	0.097
	2,400	0.207	0.152	0.125	0.081
(42X)	3,000	0.168	0.122	0.100	0.064
	3,500	0.143	0.104	0.086	0.055
	4,000	0.125	0.092	0.075	0.048
	8,000†	0.063	0.046	0.037	0.024
105 mm					
(24X)‡	16,000	0.150	0.140	0.128	0.065
(42X)	44,800	0.053	0.050	0.046	0.022
(120X)§	420,000	0.0057	0.0053	0.0049	Note ¶
(150X)§	640,000	0.0037	0.0035	0.0032	Note ¶

*Cost of in-house duplication includes basic film price, equipment rental charges, and operator labor costs, assuming full equipment and employee utilization. Since the figures in the table therefore represent an optional operating condition, costs are not likely to be lower.

†Assumes two images are laid side by side across the film.

‡Typical microfiche format used today in COM recording has 80 images at a reduction factor of 24X and 224 images at 42X.

§Microfiche having images reduced with respect to the original by factors of 100 or greater are defined as ultrafiche. At 120X, 2100 images can be held on; at 150X, 3200 images can be held.

¶Standard-grade film is assumed necessary for these magnifications.

Another popular product in COM recording is the Kodak Dacomatic®
film* These films and comparable silver halides are quite reasonably priced,
especially when compared with the finer grain varieties like Kodak AHU®
and Recordak®*, but they cost more than the duplicating films to be discussed presently. Since the master film will be used only once per report
page, its price is quite low when compared with that of paper, the alternative and its actual competitor, rather than with the duplicating films. Moreover, experience has proved its permanence.

A second outstanding property of silver halide film is its inherently
wide tonal range, which can be adjusted to meet virtually all requirements.
Third, its contrast range satisfies most specifications. Fourth, silver halide
images last so long that they are considered permanent. Indeed, more is
known from direct experience about the permanence of this film than of
any other type. For example, a film specimen actually stored for over 50
years still shows no degradation, and film stored for about 25 years without
deterioration is rather common. Libraries and governmental agencies
usually insist upon silver halide duplicates for this reason. As more direct
experience with diazo and vesicular film is acquired, more will be learned
of their aging characteristics. If this experience is consistent with the image

---

*The names Dacomatic, AHU, and Recordak are registered trade names of Eastman Kodak
Company.

Table 5-2.   Cost of Original Page and Duplicates per Report Page

NUMBER OF COPIES, ORIGINAL PLUS DUPLICATES	PAPER, CENTS	NUMBER OF FRAMES PER 100 FEET OF FILM			
		LARGE-SCALE RUN, OUT-OF-HOUSE, LOWEST QUOTATIONS, CENTS*		LOWER FILM GRADE IN-HOUSE, CENTS*	
		2000	8000	2000	8000
1	0.395	0.240	0.060	0.191	0.048
2	1.040	0.423	0.106	0.288	0.072
3	1.560	0.606	0.152	0.385	0.096
4	2.080	0.789	0.198	0.482	0.120
5	2.600	0.972	0.244	0.579	0.144
6	3.120	1.155	0.290	0.676	0.168
7	3.515	1.338	0.336	0.773	0.192
8	4.160	1.521	0.382	0.870	0.216
9	4.680	1.704	0.428	0.967	0.240
10	5.200	1.887	0.474	1.064	0.264
11	5.720	2.070	0.520	1.161	0.288
12	6.240	2.253	0.566	1.258	0.312

*High-volume run assumed in each case.

stability that these films have displayed so far, they may replace silver halides in the duplication field.

The most serious disadvantage of the silver halides is their need of relatively complicated processing. They must, of course, be run through chemical baths at moderate rates and then fed through rollers before emerging fully developed.

A second primary film type, called *diazo*, is the most widely used duplicating medium today. Its advantages over silver films are sharply lower prices and much simpler processing. A third type is thermal, or *vesicular*, film, which is also limited to duplication and is gradually overtaking diazo in popularity. It is processed even more simply than diazo and has the further advantage of undergoing tone reversal during processing. However, it costs somewhat more than diazo.

Both diazo and vesicular film are exposed by ultraviolet light rather than white visible light. In the case of diazo film, ammonia starts the development process, which continues to completion without further aid. Vesicular film needs only heat to start the image-forming process and the reintroduction of ultraviolet to stop it. Both films possess outstanding durability, owing to the use of the plastic Mylar. Diazo film never peels, but vesicular film has a tendency to do so. Both types are discussed in more detail in later sections.

If copies are to be made of the original developed film, it is put in a film duplicator to produce either diazo or thermal (e.g., Kalvar) duplicates. An unlimited number of film copies can be made at a lower cost per copy than that of the master copy, as shown in Tables 5-1 and 5-2. However, only one copy can be made at a time.

Film Costs

As an aid in calculating the monthly savings, Figure 5-1 shows a family of cost curves that compare savings for various report lengths and number of report copies. This figure is a composite of cost savings derived from displaced computer time, consumable supplies, distribution, and storage. For this analysis, computer and labor costs are assumed to be $50 per hour, report copies are distributed by mail within a radius of 150 miles, and all report copies are stored for one year.

Figure 5-1 identifies the *threshold of interest* for a potential COM user. If the user has 15 copies of a 20,000-page report to be distributed monthly, the expected cost savings would be approximately $3300 per month. Since this amount is well above the monthly rental of required equipment and operator costs for an alphanumeric COM system adequate for this application, the user should seriously consider installing such a system to handle the monthly output from this one job alone.

Figure 5-1 can also be instructive to the user with more than one large printing job. Here, the cumulative differential savings from all reports potentially diverted to COM would determine the threshold of interest. Another application of Figure 5-1 would be to postulate whether a COM system could be offered in a particular price range and then use the graph to estimate the user report load that would be needed to support acquisition of the system. For instance, if a COM system with operator could be offered for a total monthly cost of $1500, a diversion of only 50,000 original pages from the line printer (no copies) would offset the COM costs by equivalent variable cost savings.

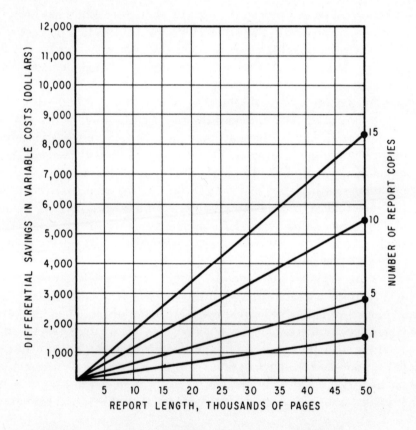

Fig. 5-1.   Variable cost differentials versus report length and
number of copies.

Generally speaking, quantity price structuring of film introduces breaks at five, ten, and similar duplication multiples, and at 500 and 1000 duplications for extremely large-scale operation. The amount of these savings is really determined by the outcome of negotiations with the supplier, and therefore the information reflected in Figure 5-1 can be only an approximation.

In view of the general unfamiliarity with diazo and vesicular film, the broadly used duplicating types, a comprehensive discussion of each now follows.

VESICULAR FILM

An important contributor to the growth of micrographics has been the process of duplication with thermal techniques. Duplication processes are critical in the micrographic chain because the end user must be satisfied with his copy. If he is not, the microform system has failed, no matter how efficient or economical it is otherwise.

As indicated previously, duplication is not accomplished with silver halide film as a rule; diazo film and the so-called thermal or dry film are more common. The term "thermal" may be used to describe a variety of different photographic processes. Dry silver, free radical imaging, heat-developed diazo, and the 3M thermal copying products are all considered thermal processes because heat acts as one of the principal processing agents. Nevertheless, it is customary to equate the word "vesicular" with thermal film; any other temperature-sensitive film will be referred to specifically. Sometimes the term "dry photography" has been used to designate vesicular film.

Images in vesicular photography begin with vesicles (microscopic bubbles) that are activated in a plastic layer. These vesicles scatter light instead of absorbing it as other photographic materials do. Thus, the vesicular image looks different to the unaided eye when compared to other photographic structures. Not infrequently, a hoary image appears, in contrast to the nonreflective black outlines of silver halide and diazo materials. This peculiarity no longer discourages users, for vesicular images seen in a viewer possess satisfactory density ranges, tonal qualities, and resolution.

Basic Principles

The agents in modern vesicular duplication are diazonium compounds that release nitrogen gas upon decomposition. These compounds are suspended in a suitable plastic coating on a transparent or opaque material. High-intensity light produces microscopic gaps in the sensitive layer by decomposing the diazonium compounds. When exposed to heat, these gaps grow into numerous microscopic bubbles that define the vesicular image. The diazonium compounds do not become part of the final image despite their similarity to diazo materials. Their sole purpose is to generate nitrogen gas that feeds the microscopic bubbles in the plastic layer. See Table 5-3.

A vesicular image is established in the area of the exposure. Normally, it is characterized by tone reversal (i.e., a negative from a positive or a positive from a negative), consistent with traditional silver halide materials. See Table 5-4. Diazo materials produce a negative from a negative or a positive from a positive, but under certain conditions, vesicular films can be dry-processed for direct-image output. This mode has been limited to special applications that justify the additional control that must be provided.

Vesicular processing requires neither the chemicals of wet processing, characteristic of silver halide films, nor ammonia as needed in diazo development. Hence, the printing and processing steps are simply exposure to ultraviolet light, development by heat, and clearing or fixing by further exposure to ultraviolet light. This process is completely dry and occurs in continuous and rapid sequence. Simple equipment operating from an electrical outlet will perform these steps.

Table 5-3. Stages of Vesicular Film Development

STAGE	CONDITION OF ACTION	CHARACTERISTIC OR RESULT
1	Plastic emulsion of crystallite particles	Stability (good shelf life)
2	Exposure to ultraviolet energy	Formation of high-pressure, latent image
3	Exposure to heat (development)	Softening of emulsion, expansion of pressure pockets, bubble image formation
4	First cooling interval	Emulsion solidification, bubble stabilization
5	Second exposure to ultraviolet energy (fixing)	Pressurization of residual crystallites
6	Second cooling interval	Escape of pressurized gas through plastic emulsion
7	Emergence of lasting bubble image in plastic form	Rugged archival microimage

Table 5-4.   Comparison of Film Types Used in Duplication

FILM TYPE	CHARACTERISTICS
Silver	All image combinations (negative to positive, positive to negative; negative to negative, positive to positive)
Diazo	Negative to negative, positive to positive
Vesicular	Negative to positive, positive to negative; negative to negative, positive to negative

Advantages

Thermal, or dry, processing has many advantages. First, printer-processors may be located in an office environment or in a computer room. Both pungent fumes and the mixing of chemical solutions are eliminated, and there is no water pollution. The dry printer-processor with automatic controls obviates pretesting for gas-chamber temperature. Indeed, dry processing dispenses entirely with chemical solutions, their cost, and their nuisance. Finally, the skills needed to operate a vesicular printer-processor are only moderately greater than those required for an office copying machine. The principles of film readability, for example, must be learned by the operator.

The tone-reversal feature of vesicular films reduces turnaround time. Most diazo films require an intermediate silver negative to produce negative copies from the original positive master. Preparation of this intermediate negative adds cost and slows delivery of copies. Even when compared to silver halide film, which also provides tone reversal, the turnaround time of vesicular film is shorter, owing to the convenience of its dry-processing feature.

Durability is another major advantage of vesicular film. Because it is coated on a polyester base, it is highly resistant to tearing, scratches, brittleness, fading, fungus, and other deterioration. However, vesicular film coating is subject to peeling, but this misfortune is seldom experienced in practice.

Further studies sponsored by Kalvar Corporation are testing image permanence of vesicular films. Data accumulated over 12 years of storage under semitropical conditions indicate that vesicular images have an extremely long life.

Of the dry-process films, vesicular films alone can be "fixed," that is, the remaining sensitive elements are completely removed by the clearing step and not just stabilized. This is important because presumably stabilized images sometimes become unstable under certain conditions.

Furthermore, vesicular films can be cleaned with soap and water without harming the image if they are accidentally splattered or contaminated with water-soluble foreign matter.

The high resolutions quoted by the vesicular film manufacturers raise an interesting point. Although the detail loss suffered in duplication is usually around 10 percent, which can certainly be considered nominal, there are occasions when the detail of the duplicate actually seems superior to the original. This phenomenon is encountered when the grain density of the master film is especially noticeable and the resolution of the duplicating film, whether vesicular or diazo, is especially high. Thus, little or no loss of inherent information occurs, and since the light-scattering property of the duplicating film types inhibits reproduction of the granular structure, the duplicate can actually give the impression of better quality than the original.

APPLICATIONS. The duplication of com-produced film is at present the principal use of vesicular films.

Film Manufacturers

At present, only three companies produce sizable quantities of vesicular films: the Kalvar Corporation, the Xidex Corporation, and Memorex Corporation. The origin of this product traces back to basic discoveries made in the early 1950s at the biophysics laboratory of Tulane University and by the Arthur D. Little Company, Cambridge, Massachusetts. In 1956 the Kalvar Corporation was organized both to manufacture a proprietary film growing out of the early research and to overcome certain practical limitations of this primitive form by developing a cheaper, more durable product. As the pioneer of the industry, Kalvar remained its sole supplier until 1970. Early in that year the slowly growing com market, for which the inherent tone reversal of vesicular film is ideally suited, led first to the founding of the Xidex Corporation and shortly afterward to the creation by Memorex of a vesicular film manufacturing facility.

Originally, Kalvar microfilms intended for com and related applications were distributed exclusively through Stromberg-DatagraphiX Supplies Division. This arrangement was quite natural in view of the near monopoly that DatagraphiX had maintained in the com industry until the recent outcropping of new companies. In June 1971, however, the relationship between the two companies was severed, and Kalvar formed its own national sales and marketing organization. A noteworthy aspect of Kalvar's marketing strategy is that it offers without charge the services of two technical support groups located at its New Orleans headquarters: the Applications Laboratory and the Systems Development Laboratory devise software and furnish other technical counsel for the client's COM installation.

Kalvar films for display systems, graphic arts, motion pictures, and aerial photography continue to be supplied directly by Kalvar or by subsidiary companies, Metro/Kalvar and Kal/Graphic.

The thermal film Xidex, introduced in 1970, is called Xidex HD, which is characterized by the usual sepia (beige) tint. In 1971 a second HD (heat developed) type was announced, Xidex HD High Speed, a blue-tinted film. According to the company, the maximum density of the blue-tinted film is achieved even in the presence of moderate density variations in the master film. Within bounds, therefore, Xidex asserts that the duplicated film will maintain an even background.

Early in 1971, Xidex and the 3M Corporation reached an agreement whereby Xidex will supply film that 3M will furnish to EBR recording system installations under a 3M Therma-Tone label.

Another recent entry into the vesicular field, Photomedia, is marketing GC 1 heat-developing film for microduplicating, positive to negative or negative to positive. It features gamma control in processing; high stability; generation printing; 3-, 4-, and 5-mil polyester and a specified resolution of 200 lines per millimeter.

The new manufacturing facilities have resulted in a total vesicular film capacity in the United States of six to seven times the current $6 million market. For this reason, observers anticipate further price decreases, even in the wake of recent drops. Specifically, a thousand feet of 16-mm film cost about $15.30 in 1970; by 1971 this price had declined to $11.25 or even $11 per thousand feet.

Duplicating Equipment

Equipment is commercially available for roll-to-roll duplication of microform images up to speeds of 200 feet per minute. With recent improvements in ultraviolet light sources, printer-processors operating at more than 300 feet per minute are possible and are in development. Presently, the manufacturers of vesicular duplicating units are Kalvar, Xidex, Memorex, Canon, Birch-Caps, and Stromberg-DatagraphiX.

Examples include the Xidex 1200 roll duplicator and the Xidex 2100 roll duplicator. The 1200, a table-top machine, will duplicate onto 16- or 35-mm Xidex HD film at rates up to 200 feet per minute. The second duplicator accepts 105-mm film and duplicates fiche formats upon it at a variable rate from 25 to 100 feet per minute. Despite its name, this machine should really be considered a sheet-to-sheet duplicator.

Other devices are available or are being designed for sheet-to-sheet microfiche duplication, aperture card duplication, and roll-to-fiche dupli-

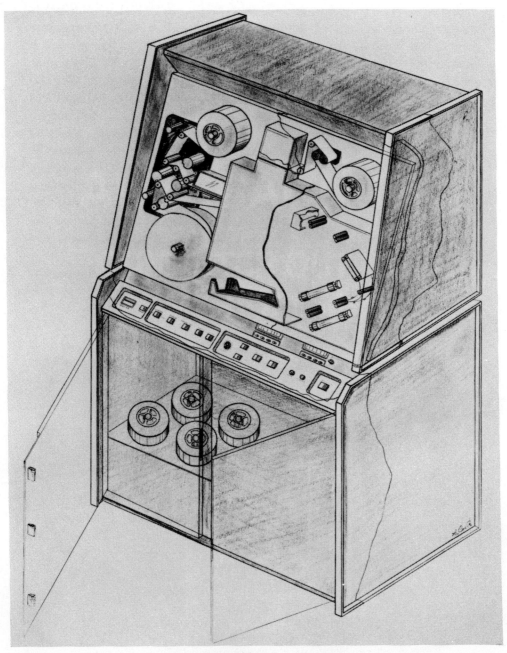

Fig. 5-2.

cation. One model, the Kalvar M-9, accepts a 4 x 6-inch sheet and reproduces it exactly at the rate of 100 fiche per hour. It has its own exposure
source, but must be supported by a separate developer. The device is
limited by the manual-operating mechanism, in contrast to the Xidex 2400,
which is automated.

Meanwhile, Kalvar has been working on two additional machines
scheduled for delivery by mid-December 1971. The Model 104 roll-to-
fiche duplicator (Fig. 5-2) will take a 105-mm roll master and, after the
operator selects a particular fiche by dialing a number, it will duplicate the
fiche onto another fiche or onto a roll. Having a built-in exposure source, a
developer, cleaner, and cutter, this automated machine drops the finished
fiche in an adjacent tray within approximately 5 seconds. A finished roll can
also be delivered when that operating mode is selected, depending on the
choice made by the operator or by the controlling program. Kalvar is also
preparing a table-top model of this device.

Figure 5-2 is an artist's drawing of the projected Model 104 duplicator.
The Kalvafiche 504 sheet-to-sheet duplicator is shown in Figure 5-3. It is
both automated and entirely self-contained.

Fig.   5-3.

Stromberg-DatagraphiX, Inc. has recently made four new roll-film duplicators available to the market: DatagraphiX Models 93, 94, 95, and 98. Each provides high-quality vesicular dry-film duplication from both positive and negative masters.

Models 93, 94, and 95 are designed for use with 16- and 35-mm film, and Model 98 duplicates microfiche recorded on 105-mm film. These duplicators need no darkroom facilities and can be used under normal office lighting.

Model 93 is a compact table-top device for medium speed, namely, 120 feet per minute. The 94, also a table-top unit, operates at 200 feet per minute.

Model 95, an upright type of device, is intended for the user who duplicates large volumes of data. It operates at speeds up to 300 feet per minute and will accept film up to 1200 feet in length for silver master and over 2000 feet for 5-mil copy film. Unlike other machines, the 95 is capable of meeting all specified performance parameters simultaneously. For example, it will duplicate 35-mm film onto the maximum size reels at the maximum speed.

Dancer arms used with each reel position allow for uniform film tension and winding, providing maximum starting speed and eliminating bad copy when starting and stopping. The 95 also features a special preexposure unit for extending the tonal range of picture or illustration duplication.

The Model 98 high-speed microfiche roll duplicator duplicates 105-mm film at speeds up to 100 feet per minute. It features upright design and utilizes a collimated light source and platenless vacuum chamber to achieve high-quality duplication at maximum throughput speed. Operator controls are kept to a minimum to allow for rapid loading, threading, duplicating, and unloading. The Model 93 offers as an option an endless film-loop unit for repetitive duplication of master films.

DatagraphiX has also announced a new, adjustable short loop attachment for the DatagraphiX 96 microfiche roll film duplicator. The loop unit adds to the versatility of the 96 by allowing for low-cost, continuous duplication of a limited number of selected fiche. The size of the loop may range from 6 to 32 fiche (3 to 16 feet).

Canon U.S.A., Inc., has announced the roll duplicator 460 for the reproduction of 105-mm or 82.5-mm microfilm on vesicular roll film in one continuous operation. Its copying rate can be as high as 60 feet per minute.

DIAZO FILM

Still more widely used than vesicular film, although being challenged increasingly, diazo film maintains its leading position as a duplicating agency by offering low cost, highly satisfactory duplicating quality, and operational simplicity. The main processing ingredient of diazo is ammonia, whereas other chemical solutions are needed for silver halides and heat is required for vesicular film. It would seem logical to conclude that vesicular film would enjoy a clear-cut preference. Nevertheless, diazo film is most popular at the present time.

Diazo Principles

The diazo coating, whether on paper or film, consists of three principal ingredients: a diazonium salt ("diazo"); one or more color bonders (couplers), often referred to as color formers; and a weak-acid stabilizer. The acidic environment interposed by the stabilizer prevents the diazonium salt and the color formers from combining into an azo dye. If the acidic environment is made alkaline through the addition of ammonia vapor, the diazonium salt and color formers will combine to produce a dye whose color is determined by the particular color-formers in the coating.

This dye spreads over the entire film surface. A dye image is propagated by superimposing a master film on diazo film and exposing the master to ultraviolet light. Its high-energy photons are absorbed in the image areas of the master, but pass through clear areas and impinge upon diazo molecules. These molecules cannot then react with the color-formers and produce a dye despite the alkaline environment.

The diazo molecules shielded from the ultraviolet light, on the other hand, can combine with the color-formers to create a dye. It is this dye that reproduces the original image (letters, numbers, lines). Since a clear area on the master produces a clear area on the duplicate, and in turn, a dark area produces a dark area, the diazo technology is called a direct, or positive, or nonreversing reproduction process.

Diazo Equipment

In the past six years, diazo duplication equipment has grown more diversified and versatile. New exposure systems have been introduced to produce more effective ultraviolet light that has increased duplicating speed. Improved tension controls in roll duplicators and improved transport control in fiche duplicators have reduced slippage. Higher-quality microcopies with greater picture detail have resulted. Developing systems have become more efficient through the use of anhydrous ammonia and more refined temperature controls. Seals have been improved to prevent ammonia leakage. Efficient loop feeders with counters for multiple-copy requirements are readily available.

Diazo duplicators that handle 16- and 35-mm roll film can achieve continuous exposure and attain development speeds ranging from 5 feet per minute to 75 feet per minute at prices from $3,500 to $25,000. High-volume production units for roll-to-roll microfiche duplication are capable of exposure/development speeds up to 100 feet per minute; these sell for $14,000 to $20,000. Card-to-roll microfiche duplicators operate at rates of 20 to 30 fiche per minute and cost $20,000 to $25,000. Card-to-card duplicators, which produce 10 to 15 fiche per minute, sell for about $10,000.

Types of Diazo Film

Presently, diazo microforms are coated in various shades of black and sepia. This choice determines the hue of the duplicated image. The advantage of sepias as intermediates is their superior ability to block ultraviolet light.

Worthy of mention is a fairly recent reversal diazo film that makes sign change possible in a procedure retaining standard diazo duplicating equipment to effect film exposure. Unfortunately, the reversal diazo film requires a separate processing step through a water bath, but despite this disadvantage it still marks a notable forward step in the diazo industry. Reversal film should be applicable in com systems calling for a negative diazo distribution copy.

Diazo Characteristics

Microimages involve three major considerations: fine detail or resolution, contrast or density, and tonal scale. All three characteristics are completely acceptable in diazo reproduction.

The small size of the diazo molecule—approximately 15 angstroms, or 200 times smaller than a silver particle—enables the fidelity of reproduction to be extremely high. Resolution loss is 10 percent or less. These diazo films are especially useful when fourth- and fifth-generation copies are required.

Contrast refers to the variation between the darkest portion (D_{max}) and the lightest portion (D_{min}) of the microfilm print. In production, diazo coatings are specified for a D_{max} as high as 2.50 and a D_{min}, or burn-out density, as low as 0.05. For normal microduplication, diazo films have a D_{max} in the vicinity of 1.80 and a D_{min} around 0.05. The high D_{max} capability of diazo can actually lead to higher contrast in a diazo copy than in the master film. Contrast is intensified by increasing the D_{max} of the diazo copy without producing an equivalent increase in the D_{min}.

Most microfilm duplication today lies in two areas: applications involving duplication of alphanumeric data for which only black-and-white reproduction is necessary, and others in which reproduction of the complete tonal range is required. The sensitometric factor that indicates ability to meet these requirements is termed "gamma." When the master has a broad tonal range, the diazo gamma should be about 1.0; for black-and-white film, gamma should be about 1.5.

To duplicate a microimage of a halftone, for example, diazo film with a gamma near 1.0 is used, since it captures all gray and beige tones as well as blacks and whites. On the other hand, if a com-type master requiring sharp black-and-white definition is to be duplicated, a higher gamma is indicated. Low-gamma films are also used for duplication of aerial reconnaissance films and for microfilm copies of engineering drawings in aperture cards.

Diazo Advantages

Because intense ultraviolet energy is needed to expose diazo films, they are not used as camera films. As a duplicating film, however, its insensitivity to light offers the advantage of letting diazo microfilm be processed in normal room light, so that no darkroom is needed. Because ammonia vapor is used for developing, there is no need for water, plumbing, chemical vats, and drying ovens. When the diazo film leaves the developer, it is dry and ready to use. Overdevelopment is impossible. The sensitometric characteristics are inherent and cannot vary during processing.

Diazo films employ both acetate and polyester bases. Thickness of the base lies between 1 and 10 mils. Polyester bases are used for applications requiring extra tensile strength. Although the acetate base is less rugged than the polyester base, it has the important property of incorporating the diazo image within the film base. Consequently, diazo-acetate films offer high resistance to scratching, fingerprinting, and soiling.

Diazo microcopies have an extremely long print life, estimated to be from 50 to over 100 years. It is said that prints over 25 years old are still in good condition.

In addition, diazo prints are not sensitive to radiation either before or after processing. Untreated diazo has higher resistance to fungus attack than do other films, even some that have received special protective treatment.

Diazo Economics

Each component of a micrographic system is extremely cost-critical. For this reason the low cost of diazo microfilm often tilts the decision of management in favor of a proposed system. It must be recognized that the greater efficiency and ease of handling of microfilm is offset by the various short-term disadvantages previously discussed. A decision for or against a microfilm system, therefore, is based primarily on economic considerations.

In evaluating a proposed COM system, for example, an analyst would compare the cost of distributing a series of computer-generated report pages to field offices with respect to paper and microfilm. He would determine the aggregate cost per page at the end points. No matter how much it costs to generate the master, this cost drops with every upward increment of duplicate copies. Indeed, as the number reaches 20, 50, 100, 500, or even more, the cost of duplication becomes more and more the dominant factor.

As a result, a diazo duplication system is increasingly regarded as the most practical means of reducing the cost per microcopy. A 100-foot roll of diazo microfilm may be duplicated for as little as $0.85, with a per-page cost of $0.003, or 3/10 mill. Similarly, a COM-generated, 200-image microfiche may be duplicated for as little as $0.045 per fiche, or 2/10 mill per page. These costs, including film-machine amortization, labor, and overhead, are the lowest offered by any duplicating technique. Indeed, it is this duality of low cost and quality that leads information managers to regard diazo as the most desirable microfilm duplication method today.

SILVER HALIDE FILM AND GENERAL CONSIDERATIONS

The fundamentals of image formation from silver halide molecules are more commonly understood than the underlying principles of the two duplicating film types. Photons releasing energy to silver compounds trigger a chemical reaction that causes the molecules to darken. If the incident light is distributed over a tonal range with respect to a determined area, the distribution defines an image that is transferred to the surface of the film in the form of activated (dark) and unactivated (light) molecules. Since incoming light, which represents bright areas of the source image, is translated into dark areas on the film, and areas receiving little light remain bright (undarkened) on the film, a tone reversal occurs. Silver halide films today produce remarkably sharp images with high contrast when correctly exposed and properly processed.

Silver halide films must be used as the original or master film produced by a COM recorder, for two main reasons. First, it is the only broad-spectrum film available; i.e., according to the silver halide salt selected, it can respond to radiant energy ranging from infrared wavelengths to ultraviolet. For CRT recorders, extended-blue Dacomatic® film is employed; and for LED recorders, extended-read Pandacomatic® is used.* (As discussed at the outset of this chapter, other silver halides are appropriate for COM as well, but the types mentioned or their equivalents are the most prevalent.) Second, only silver halides are sufficiently sensitive to react to the low-intensity illumination produced by a cathode-ray tube or photosensitive diode and to function in the short illumination periods implicit to COM recorders.

Extended-blue film is used for CRT exposure not because blue light is the only option, but rather a blue phosphor like P-11 is selected for the CRT because the most sensitive film is the extended-blue type. Similarly, diodes that emit powerfully in the infrared region are available, but the resolution and sensitivity of film filtered for response to such energy are so degraded and the properties of extended-red film are so much better that recourse to extended-red diodes is mandated. Incidentally, the inferiority of red film in comparison with blue film is amply counterbalanced by the significantly greater energy emitted by diodes as compared with that of cathode-ray tubes.

The great vexation of silver halide film is, of course, the requirement of wet, chemically treated processing in a darkroom. Adequate water and drain lines must be installed, often a formidable and expensive undertaking. In the darkroom, which is normally a sealed compartment, the film is automatically developed, stopped, fixed, washed, and dried. In addition to the chemicals, ample water must be supplied. A processing speed of 6 feet per minute is typical, but some special equipment is said to operate up to the extraordinary speed of 100 feet per minute. The delivered film has positive, black letters etched into a clear background. Since many persons opt for light letters against a dark background, there is a demand for tone reversal, and thus the particular convenience of vesicular duplicating film can be readily understood.

Functionally, there are two different types of processors. One is for positive image processing and the other for negative or "reversal" film processing. A processor is costly; for example, the Stromberg-DatagraphiX Model 89 microfilm processor lists for $6700. It has six channels, each of which processes at the rate of 5 feet per minute. For the wider 105-mm film, two rolls can be processed at a time. During processing it is possible to transform the positive image microfilm into a negative polarity by "reversal processing." Many users prefer to see negative images on their readers and to have a hard copy of a positive polarity (black printing against a light background). (*Note*: The microfilm bears a positive image because of the

---

*The name Pandacomatic is a registered trade name of Eastman Kodak Company.

tone reversal introduced by processing and the formation of a negative image on the CRT, or by LED array.)

At present, the Quantor Corporation offers three COM models having the distinction of an automatic self-contained (on-line) wet-type film processor. A built-in, sealed metal compartment acts as the darkroom. Four plastic jugs holding the necessary chemicals are installed inside the compartment, and they require replacement after 2000 feet of film, or roughly 50,000 frames, have been processed. The advantages of this feature can be considerable, especially in the case of on-line COM operation.

It will be recalled that both diazo and vesicular film must be irradiated with intense ultraviolet energy for activation. Therefore, they could never serve in the capacity of a master film. On the other hand, silver halide film, can be, and is, occasionally used as duplicating film. Its chief disadvantage in this application is price.

EQUIPMENT ROUNDUP

In late 1969 and throughout 1970 a spate of new COM units was introduced, and their effect has been to alter profoundly the character, if not the profit picture, of the industry. Whereas the historical emphasis has been on printer-plotters and graphic arts, companies like Memorex and Peripheral Technology, Inc., were perhaps the first to recognize the need for a low-cost device limited to alphanumeric printing only. They also followed the example of Kodak by eliminating the processor and depending on plugboards (Kodak's KOM-80 and KOM-90 use job-control cards) for job setup and special programming. The soundness of the concept has attracted a legion of other manufacturers into the alphanumeric field, and each has usually had a particular twist of its own.

The reader who wants to acquaint himself quickly with the various recorders now available or announced should refer to the comparison charts in Appendix I and then to the specific equipment reports of interest. If a particular equipment report has not been provided, the comparison charts should disclose another equipment of the same general kind. The combined use of the report on the other unit and the comparison chart summary on the unit of interest should convey much useful information to the reader.

Although certain aspects of four particular recorders will be briefly discussed in the subsequent paragraphs, no recommendation is implied. Indeed, the reader is reminded that numerous other interesting models have been introduced, such as the Kodak microfilmers, the CMS-5000 and

CMS-7000 of Computer Micro-Image Systems, Inc., the Beta COM series of the Beta Instruments Company and the BCOM models of the Burroughs system. In addition, there are two excellent precision graphics COM recorders on the market: the FR-80 of Information International, Inc., and the MS-5000 and MS-6000 of Singer-Link. The former is more industrially oriented, and the latter specializes in engineering and scientific applications. The Sequential S/COM-70 has already been discussed.

Memorex 1603

The distinguishing mark of the Memorex 1603 is the combination of its marketing strategy and total-system design concept. It has been presented to the data processing manager as a high-speed substitute for the IBM 1403 printer, with which it is plug-to-plug compatible. Thus, it effectively relieves the impact printers in a system setup and clears the IBM/360 main frame of congestion, whatever model it happens to be, up to the larger, high-speed system. In addition, Memorex furnishes a processor and a duplicator designed expressly for the film output of the 1603, furnishing output in the form of extremely convenient cassettes containing 100 feet of film. These cassettes snap quickly into the readers and reader-printers also provided at low cost as part of the total system. This broadly conceived, total-market approach resulted in about a 12 percent market penetration by the end of 1970. The 1603 sells for $44,250.

Quantor 1.2.3, Model 100N On-Line Microfilmer, Quantor 105

Quantor has followed the total-system idea of Memorex with an internally contained processor (optional) and high-speed readers that search automatically for specified film frames. Special cassettes have been designed as well. The 100 COM recorder, which is intended for a wider range of applications than the Memorex 1603, sells for $49,950.

A significant aspect of the 100N on-line microfilmer is the combination of an unprecedented $29,995 price tag (or $995 per month rental) with the Quantor self-contained film processor. The processor, which requires no external plumbing, delivers the first dry-film images of a run within 12 minutes of starting time.

Another distinction of the 100N is its ability to emulate the new IBM 3211 line-printer. Under program control of the host computer, the 100N stores the format image (usually entered at the computer by cards) in a buffer and thus can respond to all proper IBM control signals without the support of a plugboard or job-control cards. The 100N is therefore hardware- and software-compatible with IBM 3211 as well as with the IBM 1403 and 1443 high-speed printers. It is also fully compatible with IBM operating system and disk operating system programming. Hence, the new recorder is eminently well qualified for its intended operation, namely, as a printer for IBM/360 and IBM/370 computers.

Its console monitor displays the image as soon as it is developed on film. The 10,000 line per minute printing rate of the 100N is considered adequate for most computer operations. Experience with the Memorex 1603 has shown that this rate will usually relieve computer runs of output jam; on the other hand, exceptions to this statement have also been reported.

The 100N records on 16-mm film only, 2400 frames per 100 feet, and the film emerges already threaded on a specially designed cartridge. It is processed at the rate of 5 feet per minute. Print quality is excellent, since the characters are formed from a 7 x 10-dot matrix. Eye fatigue due to long working periods should therefore be greatly alleviated.

The internal processor can develop 2000 feet of film before requiring a new supply of chemicals. Since this length is roughly equivalent to 50,000 frames, or report pages, it represents a substantial operating period. The necessary chemicals are contained in four plastic jugs with airtight rubber plugs that prevent vaporization into the data-room atmosphere. Replacement of the old jugs by the new ones is simple and convenient, and must be carried out at least once a week.

Recording is in cine mode only. Forms flashing and retrieval mark coding are both provided. The character set, similar to OCR-B in style, consists of 64 characters. Titling can be programmed. The standard print format of 132 characters per line, 64 lines per frame, is usually produced, but scrolling (one line after another with no frame separation) is also possible.

The Quantor 105 is an off-line microfiche recorder with a built-in processor that delivers standard cut, dried microfiche at a rate of one fiche per minute, typically. This rate is equivalent to 208 pages per minute, or 12,000 an hour. The recording rate is 30,000 characters a second. Average cost per page is around 2 cents. Quantor 105 incorporates software amenable to existing operating systems so that data obtained from computer tape is recorded in the form as required by each user. That includes search, collating, editing, indexing, and formatting for automatic microfiche recording and retrieval.

The manufacturer has developed two software packages: AME, an automatic microfiche editor; and FAME, a formatting version of AME. This software has been expressly written for the IBM/360 and IBM/370 OS and DOS, and uses COBOL or other generally used languages. Functions under software control include indexing, titling, and formatting.

Fiche are cut from the film roll as they are prepared. The first fiche of a run is ready for viewing or duplicating in 4 minutes and subsequent fiche are produced at the rate of 1 per minute at average computer-page densities of 5000 to 6000 characters. The fiche are standard 4 x 5-inch positives or negatives, containing 208 pages each at a 42X reduction. The reduction may also be set to 24X, and custom reductions can be had.

The recorder operates automatically. The operator loads the computer output tape on a tape deck, inserts a job card, and, if necessary, loads a film cartridge and a Chem Pack. This last is a closed container that eliminates chemical plumbing and the conventional film processors and darkroom labs. Exhausted fluids are returned to the Chem Pack for disposal. The Quantor field service representative loads a fresh Chem Pack once a week or after 600 fiche (three cartridges of film) have been developed. The 105 recorder is said to eliminate film waste and processing delays.

The Model 105 sells for $59,950 and rents for $1750 a month, including services.

SEACO 401

To the previously described system approach, SEACO has added its own service bureaus to accommodate those who do not want an in-house installation. The 401, which sells for just under $40,000, is now marketed exclusively by Remington Rand. SEACO has also started deliveries on the Model 451 microfilmer, which is a high precision/graphic arts type of recorder.

PERTEC 3700 Computer Output Microfilmer

The PERTEC 3700 computer output microfilm printer (formerly known as the PTI-2600) is an off-line, alphanumeric, high-speed electronic printer that reads data from IBM-compatible, nine-track magnetic tape and outputs alphanumeric information in computer-page format onto microfilm. The manufacturer asserts that solid-state circuits utilizing newly available integrated-circuits chips account for the specified high printing rate of 26,000 lines per minute and for the low price. These circuits control the reading of data and the processing of input codes for driving the character generator that produces character and symbol signals. These signals generate an alphanumeric frame of 64 lines, 132 characters per line, on the face of the CRT.

Usually, the standard 64-character set of alphanumerics is provided, but an additional 26 lower-case characters are available upon request. A forms flash feature merges a preprinted form with the alphanumeric image on the microfilm. Characters can be printed in boldface. The system is set at the factory to print in comic format—that is, with lines printed along the entire length of the film—or to print in cine format, in which separate page frames are printed. The recorder has an integrated-circuit character generator for high-speed alphanumeric printing.

Data and input commands to the PERTEC 3700 are obtained from nine-track, IBM-compatible tape recorded at a density of 800 bits per inch. Input records may be blocked or unblocked with fixed or variable record length. Without an optional card reader, the maximum record length is 133 bytes, the first byte containing control information. The setup of a run is readily made by rearranging the plugs of a miniature patch panel, which controls such functions as the selection of parity, the number of lines per page, the amount of frame pulldown, the desired combination of vertical tabulations, and the selection of manual forms flash. Seven-track tape is an option. The information is written on 16-mm unsprocketed roll-film, which is available in 600- or 1000-foot magazines.

The PTI-1300 prints alphanumerics at the rate of 26,000 lines per minute when using the standard format of 64 lines per page with 132 characters per line. Depending on the information content per page, throughput may vary from 156 to 500 pages per minute. In addition to the standard computer-printout page format of 11 x 14 inches, an alternative format of 8½ x 11 inches (that limits a line to 85 characters) is available. Both formats can be programmed to allow up to 86 lines per page. The PERTEC 3700 microfilmer is priced at $59,750.

FUTURE TRENDS

In the immediate future the emphasis will be on photo-optical systems that provide more sophisticated film formatting at minimal pricing. There is a discernible trend toward reduction ratios of 42X at present and 224 frames to the 4 x 6-inch microfiche structure. It is predicted that the total system concept will become a necessity in order to minimize the cost of accessories and facilitate the acquisition of all the necessary system components by the user. Also, the role of information retrieval will gain more recognition and will be included in the total-system package. In a manner of speaking, both the Memorex approach—with its processors, duplicators, and microfilm reader series—and the Quantor approach—with its built-in processor, duplicator, and 300 series of readers—are serving this function.

APPENDIX I: COM COMPARISON CHARTS

IDENTITY		Beta Com 500	Beta Com 600	Beta Com 700
REPORT NUMBER			62.012.01	
IMAGE CHARACTERISTICS	Alphanumerics			
	Character Set	64	128	120
	Character Sizes	1	3	3
	Fonts	1	1	1
	Max Lines/Frame	64	105	105
	Brightness Levels	1	4	4
	Rotation	0°; -90°	0°; -90°	0°; -90°
	Forms Projection	Yes	Yes	Yes
	Retrieval Coding	Image Count; Code Line*	Image Count; Miracode; Code Line	Image Count; Miracode; Code Line*
	Graphics			
	Addressable Positions	N/A	4,096 x 4,096	4,096 x 4,096
INPUT	On-Line Operation	N/A	RFQ	RFQ
	Magnetic Tape			
	Channels	7 or 9	7 or 9	7 or 9
	Code	ASCII; BCD; EBCDIC	Any binary	Any binary
	Density	556, 800, 1,600* bpi	556, 800, 1,600* bpi	556, 800, 1,600* bpi
	Transfer Rate	36 kcs	36 kcs	36 kcs
	Other	—	—	—
INT CONTR PROCESSOR	Model	Format Controller	PDP-8/L	PDP-8/L
	Memory	N/A	4K	4K
	Bits per Word	N/A	12	12
	Cycle Time	N/A	1.6 msec	1.6 msec
FILM/CAMERA	Film Type	16mm; 35mm; 70mm; 105mm	16mm; 35mm	16mm; 35mm; 70mm; 105mm
	Frame Sizes	24X/17X/10X/42X reduction ratios	16mm: 0.535 x 0.535 in.; 35mm: 1.14 x 1.14 in.	24X/17X/10X/42X reduction ratios
	Frame Advance Time	75-90 msec	75-90 msec	75-90 msec
	Reel Capacity	200 ft	600 ft	200 ft

RATES	Char/Sec	36K	40K	40K
	Lines (132 char)/Min	13,000	15,000	15,000
	Throughput Std Pages/Min	220	295	295
	Graphics Points/sec	N/A	50,000 random; 100,000 incremental	50,000 random; 100,000 incremental
	Vector Plotting Time	N/A	4 msec (1 msec*)	4 msec (1 msec*)
SPECIAL FEATURES	Hard Copy	N/A	N/A	N/A
	Film Processing	Yes* (off-line)	Yes* (off-line)	Yes* (off-line)
	Other Input	—	—	—
	Other	—	—	—
OPTIONS	Mag Tape Transport	1,600 bpi	1,600 bpi; read/write	1,600 bpi; read/write
	Mag Disc	N/A	32K-128K	32K-128K
	Int Processor	N/A	N/A	N/A
	Other	—	Expanded memory; 2nd tape transport	Expanded memory; 2nd tape transport
MINIMUM PRICE		$94,000	$130,000 $3,715/mo	$153,000 $4,370/mo
COMMENTS				

N/A = Not Applicable
* Optional

IDENTITY		Burroughs BCOM B 9260	Burroughs BCOM B 9262	CalComp 900/835
REPORT NUMBER		62.016.01	62.016.01	—
IMAGE CHARACTERISTICS	Alphanumerics			
	Character Set	64	64–96	Variable
	Character Sizes	1	3	Variable
	Fonts	1	1	Variable
	Max Lines/Frame	64	64 (81*)	112
	Brightness Levels	1	1	32
	Rotation	Yes	Yes	Yes
	Forms Projection	Yes	Yes	Yes
	Retrieval Coding	No	Image count; bar code; Miracode	Yes (software controlled)
	Graphics			
	Addressable Positions	—	—	4K x 4K
INPUT	On-Line Operation	No	No	Yes
	Magnetic Tape			
	Channels	7 or 9	7 or 9	7 or 9
	Code	BCD; EBCDIC; ASCII	BCD; EBCDIC; ASCII	Binary
	Density	200, 556, 800 bpi	200, 556, 800 bpi	200, 556, 800 bpi
	Transfer Rate	50 kcs	50–96 kcs	30 kcs
	Other	—	—	—
INT CONTR PROCESSOR	Model	—	—	CalComp
	Memory	—	—	4–32K
	Bits Per Word	—	—	9
	Cycle Time	—	—	2 μsec
FILM/CAMERA	Film Type	16mm	16mm; 105mm	16mm; 35mm
	Frame Sizes	0.567 x 0.567 in.	0.567 x 0.567 in.	0.405 x 0.526 in.; 1.13 x 1.43 in.
	Frame Advance Time	80 msec	80 msec	100 msec
	Reel Capacity	1,000 ft	1,000 ft (16 mm) 200 ft (105 mm)	400 ft

RATES	Char/Sec	50K	50–96K	2.7K
	Lines (132 char)/Min	22,080	22,080–43,620	2,400
	Throughput Std Pages/Min	241	241–466	24
	Graphics Points/sec	—	—	140K
	Vector Plotting Time	—	—	7 μsec to 14 msec (length dependent)
SPECIAL FEATURES	Hard Copy	No	Yes; Polaroid camera	No
	Film Processing	No	No	No
	Other Input	—	—	On-line
	Other	—	—	—
OPTIONS	Mag Tape Transport	Yes	Yes	Yes
	Mag Disc	No	No	Yes
	Int Processor	—	No	Yes
	Other	—	—	Remote terminal
MINIMUM PRICE		$85,000	$85,000	$90,000
COMMENTS		No longer marketed		A storage-tube visual monitor is included.

* Optional

		CalComp 835	CalComp 1670	Canon J-COM 202
IDENTITY				
REPORT NUMBER		—	—	—
IMAGE CHARACTERISTICS	Alphanumerics			
	Character Set	Variable	Variable	192
	Character Sizes	Variable	Variable	Selectable
	Fonts	Variable	1	Selectable
	Max Lines/Frame	112	112	64
	Brightness Levels	32	32	1
	Rotation	Yes	Yes	No
	Forms Projection	Yes (programmable)	Optional	Yes
	Retrieval Coding	Yes (software controlled)	Miracode; sequential retrieval mark	Image Count
	Graphics			
	Addressable Positions	4K x 4K	16K x 16K	—
INPUT	On-Line Operation	Yes	Yes	Yes
	Magnetic Tape			
	Channels	7 or 9	7 or 9	7 or 9
	Code	Binary	Binary	Any
	Density	200, 556, 800 bpi	200, 556, 800, 1,600 bpi	556, 800 bpi
	Transfer Rate	30 kcs	30 kcs	20–60 kcs
	Other	—	—	—
INT CONTR PROCESSOR	Model	CalComp	CalComp 900	—
	Memory	Tape read only	4K–32K	2K
	Bits per Word	—	9	12
	Cycle Time	—	2 μsec	3 μsec
FILM/CAMERA	Film Type	16mm; 35mm	16mm; 35mm; 105mm	16mm, 35mm*, 82.55mm*, 105mm*
	Frame Sizes	0.405 x 0.526 in.; 1.13 x 1.43 in.	0.405 x 0.526 in.; 1.13 x 1.43 in.	13 x 6.9; 8.7; 13.9; 15.2 inches
	Frame Advance Time	100 msec	50–100 msec	75 msec
	Reel Capacity	400 ft	400 ft	600; 1,200 ft

RATES	Char/Sec	2.6K	10K/30K (see Comments)	25K
	Lines (132 char)/Min	1,200	4,500/10,000 (see Comments)	9,300
	Throughput Std Pages/Min	17	66 (see Comments)	145
	Graphics Points/sec	100K	500K	—
	Vector Plotting Time	10 μsec to 20 msec (length dependent)	2 μsec to 8 msec (length dependent)	—
SPECIAL FEATURES	Hard Copy	No	Yes	No
	Film Processing	No	No	Yes (16mm)
	Other Input	—	On-line	—
	Other	—	—	Monitor
OPTIONS	Mag Tape Transport	Yes	Yes	Yes
	Mag Disc	No	Yes	Yes
	Int Processor	Yes	Yes	No
	Other	—	Remote terminal	—
MINIMUM PRICE		$50,000	$120,000	$100,000
COMMENTS		A storage-tube visual monitor is included for direct viewing.	Higher output obtained with optional hardware character generator. A storage-tube visual monitor is included. A microfiche capability is available.	

* Optional

IDENTITY		CMS-7000	DatagraphiX 4020	DatagraphiX 4060
REPORT NUMBER		62.110.01	—	62.088.02
IMAGE CHARACTERISTICS	Alphanumerics			
	Character Set	64-128	62	127
	Character Sizes	48	1	4
	Fonts	3	1	1
	Max Lines/Frame	128	88	100
	Brightness Levels	2	Up to 16*	4
	Rotation	Yes	No	Yes
	Forms Projection	Yes (see Comments)	Yes	Yes
	Retrieval Coding	Image count; Miracode; code line	Sequential retrieval mark	See Comments
	Graphics			
	Addressable Positions	—	1K x 1K	4K x 3K
INPUT	On-Line Operation	No	No	Yes
	Magnetic Tape			
	Channels	7 or 9	7 or 9	7 or 9
	Code	Any	EBC; EBCDIC	BCD; EBCDIC; ASCII
	Density	200, 556, 800, 1,600 bpi	200, 556, 800 bpi	556, 800 bpi
	Transfer Rate	240 kcs	17 kcs	256 kcs
	Other	1,600 bpi*	—	—
INT CONTR PROCESSOR	Model	Computer Micro-Image	—	Honeywell 516
	Memory	4 - 32K	—	8K
	Bits Per Word	16	—	16
	Cycle Time	1 μsec	—	960 μsec
FILM/CAMERA	Film Type	16mm; 35mm; 105mm	16 mm; 35mm	16mm; 35mm
	Frame Sizes	Variable	Dependent on camera and lens	Dependent on camera and lens
	Frame Advance Time	20 msec	100 msec	100 msec
	Reel Capacity	100, 600, 1,000 ft	600 ft	600 ft

RATES	Char/Sec	67–188K	17K	40K
	Lines (132 char)/Min	50,000	7,000	9,000
	Throughput Std Pages/Min	270/900 (min/max)	100	135/600 (min/max)
	Graphics Points/sec	—	17.8K	60K
	Vector Plotting Time	—	300 μsec (length dependent)	4 msec (depends on resolution)
SPECIAL FEATURES	Hard Copy	No	Yes	Yes
	Film Processing	No	No	Yes
	Other Input	—	—	On-line
	Other	Memory expansion	—	—
OPTIONS	Mag Tape Transport	Yes	No	Yes
	Mag Disc	No	No	No
	Int Processor	Double 4K modules to 32K	—	No
	Other	On-line interface; see report	—	On-line
MINIMUM PRICE		$110,000	$154,960	$275,000
COMMENTS		System can be operated off-line from magnetic tape. Information being printed displayed on monitor CRT. Form projection effected by 8-cell carousel. Microfiche has up to 500 images.		Available retrieval coding includes image count, Miracode, code line, sequential retrieval mark.

* Optional

IDENTITY		DatagraphiX 4360	Datagraphix 4400	Ferranti ADE Microfilm Plotter EP 140
REPORT NUMBER		62,088.03		
IMAGE CHARACTERISTICS	Alphanumerics			
	Character Set	64	64	94
	Character Sizes	1	1	2
	Fonts	1	1	1
	Max Lines/Frame	64	76	—
	Brightness Levels	1	1	1
	Rotation	Yes	Yes	Via software
	Forms Projection	Yes	Yes	Yes*
	Retrieval Coding	Sequential retrieval mark	See Comments	No
	Graphics			
	Addressable Positions	N/A	N/A	16K x 16K
INPUT	On-Line Operation	No	No	Yes
	Magnetic Tape			
	Channels	7 or 9	7 or 9	7 or 9
	Code	EBC; EBCDIC	EBC; EBCDIC	ASCII
	Density	556, 800, 1,600 bpi	200, 556, 800 bpi	200, 556, 800, 1,600 bpi
	Transfer Rate	60 kcs	60 kcs	30 kcs
	Other	N/A	N/A	—
INT CONTR PROCESSOR	Model	N/A	N/A	N/A; PDP-8/L*
	Memory	N/A	N/A	—
	Bits Per Word	N/A	N/A	—
	Cycle Time	N/A	N/A	—
FILM/CAMERA	Film Type	16mm; 105mm	16mm	16mm; 35mm
	Frame Sizes	Dependent on camera and lens	Dependent on camera and lens	0.295 x 0.409 in.; 0.709 x 0.945 in.
	Frame Advance Time	254 msec	100 msec	1 sec to 45 sec (see Comments)
	Reel Capacity	100 ft (cassette); 200 ft (mag)	600; 1,000 ft	200 ft; 500 cards

		Product 1	Product 2	Product 3
RATES	Char/Sec	60K	60K	500
	Lines (132 char)/Min	10,000	15,000	200
	Throughput Std Pages/Min	111	250	2
	Graphics Points/sec	N/A	N/A	500K
	Vector Plotting Time	N/A	N/A	100 msec (full width)
SPECIAL FEATURES	Hard Copy	No	No	No
	Film Processing	No	No	For aperture cards
	Other Input	N/A	N/A	Paper tape*
	Other	—	—	—
OPTIONS	Mag Tape Transport	Yes	Yes	Yes
	Mag Disc	No	No	No
	Int Processor	N/A	N/A	No
	Other	Universal camera	N/A	CRT monitor
MINIMUM PRICE		$69,000	$83,200	$60,000
COMMENTS			Available retrieval coding includes Image Count, Miracode, Code Line, sequential retrieval mark.	The standard output is 35mm aperture cards.

N/A — Not Applicable
* Optional

	IDENTITY	Ferranti ADE Microfilm Plotter EP 240	Information International FR-80	KODAK KOM-90 Microfilmer
	REPORT NUMBER		62.058.01	62.034.01
IMAGE CHARACTERISTICS	**Alphanumerics**			
	Character Set	94	90; 128*	64 std; 121 opt
	Character Sizes	2	64	2
	Fonts	1	Variable	4
	Max Lines/Frame	—	Not available	64
	Brightness Levels	1	8	2
	Rotation	Via software*	Yes (see Comments)	Yes (see Comments)
	Forms Projection	Yes*	No, but form superposition is possible	Yes
	Retrieval Coding	No	Image Count; Bar Code; Miracode	Image Count; Miracode; Code Line
	Graphics			
	Addressable Positions	16K x 16K	16K x 16K	—
INPUT	On-Line Operation	Yes	Yes*	No
	Magnetic Tape			
	Channels	7 or 9	7 or 9	7 or 9
	Code	ASCII	Binary; BCD; EBCDIC	BCD, EBCDIC
	Density	200, 556, 800, 1,600 bpi	200, 556, 800 bpi	200, 556, 800 bpi; 1,600 bpi (see Comments)
	Transfer Rate	30 kcs	Not available	90K char/sec (up to 120K char/sec)
	Other	—	45 ips	112.5 ips (tape transfer rate)
INT CONTR PROCESSOR	Model	N/A; PDP-8/L*	DEC PDP-9/L — PDP-15	—
	Memory	—	4–32K	
	Bits per Word	—	18	
	Cycle Time	—	1 μsec	
FILM/CAMERA	Film Type	16mm; 35mm	16mm; 35mm perf & unperf; 105mm	16mm (unperf); also 35, 82.5, and 105mm
	Frame Sizes	0.295 x 0.409 in.; 0.709 x 0.945 in.	0.295 x 0.404 in.; 0.748 x 0.980 in.; etc.	0.372 x 0.46 (28x); 0.46 x 0.57 (23x)
	Frame Advance Time	100 msec	74 msec	Less than 100 msec
	Reel Capacity	500 ft	Not available	600 ft; 1,000 ft

RATES	Char/Sec	12,000	15K-100K* (see Comments)	90K char/sec (up to 120K char/sec)
	Lines (132 char)/Min	5,000	3,600/18,000 (see Comments)	41,000 (up to 54,000)
	Throughput Std Pages/Min	175	53/250 (min/max) (see Comments)	350 (see Comments)
	Graphics Points/sec	500K	100K	—
	Vector Plotting Time	100 msec (full width)	1 msec	
SPECIAL FEATURES	Hard Copy	No	No	None
	Film Processing	No	No	
	Other Input	Paper tape*	Light pen; ASR 33 Teletype	
	Other	—	Line and paragraph spacing; right and left justification	
OPTIONS	Mag Tape Transport	Yes (std)	No	Yes
	Mag Disc	No	Yes	No
	Int Processor	No	Expandable to 32K	No
	Other	CRT monitor	N/A	No
MINIMUM PRICE		Available from manufacturer	$225,000	$88,000
COMMENTS			Possible orientations are 0°, 45°, 90°, 135°, 180°, 225°, 270°, 315°. Higher output with optional hardware character generator. Capable of limited phototypesetting. Excellent optical system. Excellent graphic capabilities.	Recording modes are cine, comic, reverse cine, reverse comic; each related pair available for each frame size as specified on JSCC; NRZI recorded up to 800 bpi; phase encoded at 1,600 bpi; throughput based on advance time of 100 msec and 120K char/sec transfer rate.

N/A — Not Applicable
* Optional

IDENTITY		Singer–Link APD–5000	Memorex 1603	Peripheral Technology Inc. PTI–1300
REPORT NUMBER		62.045.01	62.109.01	62.108.01
IMAGE CHARACTERISTICS	Alphanumerics	60 (more programmable)	64	64-90*
	Character Set	Hdwe: fixed; sfwe: variable	1	1
	Character Sizes	1	1	1
	Fonts	300	64 plus scrolling	86
	Max Lines/Frame	8	1	2
	Brightness Levels	By programming	—	No
	Rotation	Yes*	Yes	Yes*
	Forms Projection	Miracode*	No	Bar code; Miracode; code line; image count
	Retrieval Coding			
	Graphics			
	Addressable Positions	16K x 12K	—	—
INPUT	On-Line Operation	Yes	Yes	No
	Magnetic Tape			
	Channels	7 or 9		9
	Code	Binary	EBCDIC	EBCDIC; NRZI
	Density	556, 800 bpi		800 bpi
	Transfer Rate	100 kcs	Up to 500 kcs	30 kcs
	Other	—	—	37.5 ips
INT CONTR PROCESSOR	Model	—	—	—
	Memory	—	—	—
	Bits per Word	—	—	—
	Cycle Time	—	—	—
FILM/CAMERA	Film Type	16mm; 35mm perf and unperf	16mm	16mm
	Frame Sizes	16mm: 0.77 x 0.58 in.; 35mm: 1.6 x 1.2 in.	0.410 x 0.630 in.; 0.500 x 0.630 in.	0.44 x 0.55 in
	Frame Advance Time	100 msec	28 msec	80 msec
	Reel Capacity	400, 600, 1,000 ft	500 ft	600, 1,000 ft

RATES	Char/Sec	Hdwe: 17K; sfwe: 2K (see Comments)	22K	30K
	Lines (132 char)/Min	Hdwe: 7,700; sfwe: 900 (see Comments)	10,000	13,000
	Throughput Std Pages/Min	85–180 (see Comments)	145	156
	Graphics Points/sec	100K	—	—
	Vector Plotting Time	2–4 msec (depends on resolution)	—	—
SPECIAL FEATURES	Hard Copy	No	Yes*	No
	Film Processing	No	Yes*	No
	Other Input	On-line	—	No
	Other	Variable lenses; film magazines	Sealed display assembly	Normal or dark print mode
OPTIONS	Mag Tape Transport	Yes	No	Yes (7-track)
	Mag Disc	No	No	No
	Int Processor	—	—	—
	Other	Storage-tube display; hardware character generator	Hard copy from 1650 Viewer/Printer	Dump mode; card reader 42X reduction ratio
MINIMUM PRICE		$114,950	$44,250	$49,750
COMMENTS		Higher output with optional hardware character generator. System designed primarily for graphic plotting; can generate many useful forms. See report. Plotting time of a graphic form is typically 1–2 seconds.	Image formed by a matrix of photo-diodes and associated fiber optic strands; need for digital-to-analog conversion thereby avoided. Lines for standard frame and scrolling printed at 156 lines/inch.	No longer marketed

* Optional

IDENTITY		Pertec 3700	Scan Graphics GraphiCOM	SEACO COM Reader Model 401
REPORT NUMBER		62.108.01	62.113.01	—
IMAGE CHARACTERISTICS	Alphanumerics			
	Character Set	64-90*	128	64
	Character Sizes	2	8	Variable
	Fonts	1	1	1
	Max Lines/Frame	86	—	64
	Brightness Levels	Operator controlled	8	1
	Rotation	No	Yes *(variable)	Yes
	Forms Projection	Yes*	Yes*	Yes
	Retrieval Coding	Code line; image count	Image count; Miracode; code line	No
	Graphics			
	Addressable Positions	—	16K x 16K	—
INPUT	On-Line Operation	No	Yes	Yes
	Magnetic Tape			
	Channels	9	7 or 9	7 or 9
	Code	EBCDIC, BCD, ASCII	Any	EBC; EBCDIC
	Density	556, 800, 1,600 bpi	556; 800 bpi	556; 800; 1,600 bpi
	Transfer Rate	60 kcs	40 kcs	36 kcs
	Other	—	1,600 bpi*	—
INT CONTR PROCESSOR	Model	—	DEC PDP-15	—
	Memory	—	8-32K	—
	Bits per Word	—	18	—
	Cycle Time	—	800 msec	—
FILM/CAMERA	Film Type	16mm; 35mm; 70mm; 105mm	16mm; 35mm; 105mm	16mm
	Frame Sizes	0.44 x 0.55 in. (16mm)	1.133 x 1.467 in. (35mm unperf); 0.709 x 0.945 in. (35mm perf); 0.440 x 0.561 (16mm unperf)	Variable
	Frame Advance Time	120 msec	100 msec	75 msec
	Reel Capacity	600, 1,000 ft	1,000 ft	600 ft

RATES	Char/Sec	60K	10K; 40K*	36K
	Lines (132 char)/Min	26,000	18,000	16,355
	Throughput Std Pages/Min	240	191	195
	Graphics Points/sec	—	500K	—
	Vector Plotting Time	—	1 msec	—
SPECIAL FEATURES	Hard Copy	No	No	No
	Film Processing	No	No	No
	Other Input	No	Paper tape	—
	Other	Normal or dark print mode	—	—
OPTIONS	Mag Tape Transport	Yes (9-track)	Yes	7- or 9-track
	Mag Disc	No	Yes	No
	Int Processor	—	Expandable to 32K	—
	Other	Dump mode; card reader; 42X reduction ratio	Special fonts	—
MINIMUM PRICE		$59,750	$215,000	$39,850
COMMENTS		Retrieval coding is an option. System is factory set for comic printout but cine format can be ordered. There are 4 operator-selectable frame sizes.	Scan Graphics is now defunct.	

* Optional

IDENTITY		3M Series "F" EBR	DatagraphiX 4200	DatagraphiX 4440
REPORT NUMBER		62.097.02		62.088.04
IMAGE CHARACTERISTICS	Alphanumerics			
	Character Set	60 (plus 64 opt)	64	64-128
	Character Sizes	3	1	1
	Fonts	1 (uc and lc)	1	1
	Max Lines/Frame	64	64	76
	Brightness Levels	2	1	1
	Rotation	Yes	Yes (see Comments)	Yes
	Forms Projection	Yes*	Yes (see Comments)	Yes
	Retrieval Coding	Image Count (3M Page Search Blip)	Sequential retrieval mark	Image Count; Miracode; Code Line; sequential retrieval mark
	Graphics			
	Addressable Positions	2K x 2K	N/A	N/A
INPUT	On-Line Operation	See Comments	Yes (IBM 360 Models 25 and up)	Yes
	Magnetic Tape		N/A	
	Channels	7 or 9		7 or 9
	Code	7-track: BCD, NRZI; 9-track: EBCDIC		EBC, EBCDIC
	Density	200, 556, 800, 1,600* bpi		556, 800, 1,600 bpi
	Transfer Rate	15/41.7/60 kcs	60 kcs	120 kcs
	Other	75 ips	—	N/A
INT CONTR PROCESSOR	Model	3M/CDC/Lockheed	N/A	N/A
	Memory	4-32K	N/A	N/A
	Bits per Word	16	N/A	N/A
	Cycle Time	1 μsec	N/A	N/A
FILM/CAMERA	Film Type	16mm	16mm; 35mm; 105mm	16mm; 105mm
	Frame Sizes	0.551 x 0.551 in.; 0.276 x 0.276 in.	24X: 0.427 x 0.528 42X: 0.254 x 0.314	Dependent on camera and lens
	Frame Advance Time	25-60 msec	150 msec	100 msec
	Reel Capacity	675 ft (normal)	200 ft	200 ft, 600 ft, 1000 ft

RATES	Char/Sec	60K (max)	60K	120K
	Lines (132 char)/Min	20,000	13,000	30,000
	Throughput Std Pages/Min	395	240	340
	Graphics Points/sec	40K	N/A	N/A
	Vector Plotting Time	150 μsec (corner to corner)		
SPECIAL FEATURES	Hard Copy	Yes	No	No
	Film Processing	Yes	No	No
	Other Input	N/A	No	On-line
	Other	—	—	—
OPTIONS	Mag Tape Transport	Yes	No	Yes
	Mag Disc	Yes	No	No
	Int Processor	4K memory increments; 9-track tape; software packages	No	N/A
	Other	—	—	Universal camera
MINIMUM PRICE		$86,600 (with necessary components, $105,000)	$49,000	$108,000
COMMENTS		Image on microfilm formed by direct impact of focused electron beam; on-line operation of system upon request only.	Full software support to adapt 4200 to any output mode of 360 operation. All system features, including Universal camera, are standard. Charactron CRT can be physically rotated for cine or comic output.	

N/A — Not Applicable
* Optional

IDENTITY		Quantor 100 Series Microfilm Recorder	Alpha-Vector AV-2000 Computer Micro-Image Recorder	KODAK KOM-80 Microfilmer
REPORT NUMBER				62.034.08
IMAGE CHARACTERISTICS	Alphanumerics			
	Character Set	64	64 or 96 (user specifies)	64 std; 82 opt
	Character Sizes	1	1	2
	Fonts	1	1	4
	Max Lines/Frame	64	76	64
	Brightness Levels	1	1	2
	Rotation	No (see Comments)	Yes	Yes (see Comments)
	Forms Projection	Yes	Yes	Yes
	Retrieval Coding	Image Count	AVector Code; Miracode; Image Count	Image Count; Miracode*; Code Line*
	Graphics			—
	Addressable Positions	N/A	N/A	
INPUT	On-Line Operation	No	Yes	No
	Magnetic Tape		See Comments	
	Channels	9		9
	Code	EBCDIC, NRZI recorded		EBCDIC
	Density	800 bpi		800 bpi; 1,600 bpi (see Comments)
	Transfer Rate	19,200 bytes/sec	500 kcs	90K char/sec (up to 120K char/sec)
	Other			112.5 ips (tape transfer rate)
INT CONTR PROCESSOR	Model	N/A	AV-236	—
	Memory		2K	
	Bits Per Word		8	
	Cycle Time		250 nsec	
FILM/CAMERA	Film Type	16mm unperforated	16mm unperforated (see Comments)	16mm (unperf); also 35, 82.5, and 105mm
	Frame Sizes	0.393 x 0.500 (min); 0.408 x 0.519 (max)	0.528 (144 char) x 0.426 (76 lines) in. at 24X; 0.302 (144 char) x 0.244 (76 lines) in.	0.372 x 0.46; 0.46 x 0.57
	Frame Advance Time	30 msec	10 msec (max)	Less than 100 msec
	Reel Capacity	400 ft	1,000 ft	600 ft; 1,000 ft

RATES	Char/Sec	19,200	218,880	90K char/sec (up to 120K char/sec)
	Lines (132 char)/Min	21,000	91,200	41,000 (up to 54,000)
	Throughput Std Pages/Min	300 (range: 110–590)	1,200	350 (see Comments)
	Graphics Points/sec	N/A	N/A	—
	Vector Plotting Time			
SPECIAL FEATURES	Hard Copy	No	No	None
	Film Processing	Yes*		
	Other Input	No		
	Other	Card reader; dump mode		
OPTIONS	Mag Tape Transport	—	N/A	Yes
	Mag Disc	No	No	No
	Int Processor	No	N/A	No
	Other	Built-in film processor; software according to needs	No (see Comments)	No
MINIMUM PRICE		$49,500	$49,750	$68,700
COMMENTS		Accepts input tape with block format. Optional built-in film processor requires no external plumbing; all chemicals internally contained. Cine or comic mode output preset as specified by user. Optional software available to adapt any designated input format to system. Manufacturer attributes high throughput to rapid camera action, in particular; 30 msec frame advance time. Job selection control card fixes output format (standard). Recorder is part of Quantor Microfilm Information System.	Manufacturer estimates first delivery will be in February 1971. First delivered systems will interface with IBM 360 Models 25 and up; later systems will interface with other principal computers as designated by user. Off-line system AV-3000 scheduled for second quarter of 1971. Modular optional 105mm camera with reduction of 150X scheduled for first quarter of 1971. All features of system, except 105mm camera when available, are standard. Output recorded in cine or comic mode as commanded by computer program.	Recording modes are cine, comic, reverse cine, reverse comic; user may specify 1 of a pair for each of 2 frame sizes; NRZI encoded at 800 bpi, phase encoded at 1,600 bpi; throughput based on frame advance time of 100 msec and 120K char/sec transfer rate.

N/A — Not Applicable
* Optional

IDENTITY		Sequential Information S/COM-70, Model 1	Sequential Information S/COM-70, Model 2	
REPORT NUMBER				
IMAGE CHARACTERISTICS	Alphanumerics			
	Character Set	64 (expandable to 128)	64 (expandable to 128)	
	Character Sizes	1	1	
	Fonts	1	1	
	Max Lines/Frame	64	64	
	Brightness Levels	1	1	
	Rotation	No	No	
	Forms Projection	Yes	Yes	
	Retrieval Coding	Miracode*; Image Count*; Index Line*	Miracode*; Image Count*; Index Line*	
	Graphics			
	Addressable Positions	924 x 768	924 x 768	
INPUT	On-Line Operation	IBM/360 Models 25 and up	No	
	Magnetic Tape	N/A		
	Channels		9	
	Code		EBCDIC; BCD*; ASCII*	
	Density		800 bpi; 200 and 556 bpi*	
	Transfer Rate	500 kcs	30 kcs	
	Other	Interfaces for other principal computers available	7-track tape* (with lower densities above); 9-track with 1,600 bpi	
INT CONTR PROCESSOR	Model	N/A	N/A	
	Memory			
	Bits per Word			
	Cycle Time			
FILM/CAMERA	Film Type	16mm unperforated	16mm unperforated	
	Frame Sizes	0.528 x 0.425 in.	0.528 x 0.425 in.	
	Frame Advance Time	6 msec (see Comments)	6 msec (see Comments)	
	Reel Capacity	600 ft	600 ft	

RATES	Char/Sec	33 kcs	33 kcs
	Lines (132 char)/Min	15,000	13,500
	Throughput Std Pages/Min	226	210
	Graphics Points/sec	500K (incremental); 2.3M (continuous)	500K (incremental); 2.3M (continuous)
	Vector Plotting Time	N/A	N/A
SPECIAL FEATURES	Hard Copy	No	No
	Film Processing		
	Other Input		
	Other		
OPTIONS	Mag Tape Transport	No	7-track
	Mag Disc	No	No
	Int Processor	No	No
	Other	No	No
MINIMUM PRICE		$37,500	$37,500
COMMENTS		Image of both models formed on light-emitting diode array (LED). Need for high-precision circuits associated with CRT displays thereby eliminated. 105mm fiche capability, standard formats; recording in comic mode. Recording on film is line by line, with film incremented after completion of each line; at end of frame film is advanced about six lines to start of next frame; this technique contributes to short equivalent pulldown time; recording on 16mm film in cine mode. Forms overlay positioned alongside diode array; photographed separately and superimposed on display image recorded on film; precision in forms overlay unnecessary. Precision required only of photo-optical system, which executes stable intervals and maintains constant pitch. Programmable plug board emulates carriage control tape of 1403 or 1443 Line Printers. Manufacturer expects to market primarily on OEM basis, but not exclusively. Manufacturer has scheduled first delivery of system for second quarter of 1971.	

N/A — Not Applicable
* Optional

IDENTITY			Singer-Link MS-6000 Series
REPORT NUMBER			
IMAGE CHARACTERISTICS	Alphanumerics		
		Character Set	60; 100 (both ASCII and EBCDIC codes)
		Character Sizes	8
		Fonts	1
		Max Lines/Frame	64
		Brightness Levels	1
		Rotation	90°
		Forms Projection	Manual slide; 63-unit auto-slide; software generated
		Retrieval Coding	Miracode (14 Bar)
	Graphics		
		Addressable Positions	206 x 106
INPUT	On-Line Operation		Yes
	Magnetic Tape		Yes
		Channels	7; 9
		Code	Any
		Density	556; 800
	Transfer Rate		600 kcs on-line
	Other		240 kcs off-line
INT CONTR PROCESSOR	Model		MS-6010 MS-6020 MS-6030
	Memory		4-32K 8-64K 8-64K
	Bits per Word		24 24 24
	Cycle Time		1.2 µsec 1.0 µsec 0.6 µsec
FILM/CAMERA	Film Type		105mm (fiche); 16mm, 35mm (roll film)
	Frame Sizes		1.433" x 1.1" max (35mm); NMA A1 8-1/2" x 11" (105mm film); 0.583" x 0.583" max (16mm); NMA A3 11" x 14"
	Frame Advance Time		100 msec
	Reel Capacity		400', 600', 1,000' (16mm/35mm); 100' (105mm)

RATES	Char/Sec	20,000
	Lines (132 char)/Min	8,050
	Throughput Std Pages/Min	115 (including frame advance)
	Graphics Points/sec	100,000
	Vector Plotting Time	See Comments
SPECIAL FEATURES	Hard Copy	No
	Film Processing	No
	Other Input	No
	Other	Extensive graphics package; complete conversion for most plotter formats; applications package
OPTIONS	Mag Tape Transport	High-speed drive
	Mag Disc	Yes
	Int Processor	Standard
	Other	Character generator; forms flash
MINIMUM PRICE		Consult manufacturer
COMMENTS		Scheduled for delivery in 1971.
		Two hardware generators are available, with the 60-symbol generator standard. Both codes are compatible with the optional generator as indicated above.
		Software is a standard feature.
		Fonts are available with complete flexibility in rotation and aspect ratio; 8 intensities and 8 line widths.
		Vector plotting time depends upon intensity selected and type of film used; also depends upon length of vector.

APPENDIX II: COM MANUFACTURERS

The following companies produce readers for displaying microfilm or microfiche. Some readers are especially designed for COM formats.

Arcata Microfilm Corp., 700 South Main St., Spring Valley, N. Y. 10977

Atlantic Technology Corp., Somers Point Shopping Center, Somers Point, N. J. 08244

Bell and Howell, Micro-Data Division, 6800 McCormick Rd., Chicago, Ill. 60645

Beta Instrument Corp., 20 Ossippee Rd., Newton Upper Falls, Mass. 02164

Burroughs Corp., 6071 Second Ave., Detroit, Mich. 48232

California Computer Products, Inc., 305 North Muller St., Anaheim, Calif. 92803

Canon U.S.A., Inc., 64-10 Queens Blvd., Woodside, N. Y. 11377

Computer Micro-Image Systems, Inc., 9600 DeSoto Ave., Chatsworth, Calif. 91311

DASA Corp., 15 Stevens St., Andover, Mass. 01810

Eastman Kodak Co., Business Systems Markets Division, 343 State St., Rochester, N. Y. 14650

Ednalite Corp., Memory Display Systems Division, 200 North Water St., Peekskill, N. Y. 10566

Eugene Dietzgen Co., 2425 North Sheffield Ave., Chicago, Ill.

Ferranti Electric, Inc., East Bethpage Rd., Plainview, N. Y. 11803

Itek Business Products, Itek Corp., Rochester, N. Y. 14603

Keuffel & Esser Co., 20 Whippany Rd., Morristown, N. J. 07960

Memorex Corp., 1180 Shulman Ave., Santa Clara, Calif. 95052

Microfilm Products, Inc., 40 West 15th St., New York, N. Y. 10011

Micro-Scan Systems, Inc., 54 South Main St., Pearl River, N. Y. 10965

Minolta Corp., 200 Park Avenue South, New York, N. Y. 10003

The National Cash Register Co., Industrial Products Division, Dayton, Ohio 45409

Pertec Business Systems, 17112 Armstrong Ave., Santa Ana, Calif. 92705

Quantor, 10950 N. Tantau Ave., Cupertino, Calif. 95014

SEACO Computer-Display Inc., 2714 National Circle, Garland, Texas 75040

Sequential Information Systems, Inc., 249 North Saw Mill River Rd., Elmsford, N. Y. 10523

The Singer Co., Singer-Link Division, 1077 East Arques Ave., Sunnyvale, Calif. 94086

Stromberg-DatagraphiX, Inc., P.O. Box 2449, San Diego, Calif. 92112

Teledyne Frederick Post, Box 803, Chicago, Ill. 60690

3M Co., 3M Center, St. Paul, Minn. 55101

University Computing Co. (formerly Computer Industries, Inc.), Graphic Systems Division, 14761 Califa St., Van Nuys, Calif. 91401

Washington Scientific Industries, Inc., Long Lake, Minn. 55356

GLOSSARY

Aberration. Any deviation from point-to-point correspondence between an object and its image as formed by an optical or an electronic system, or between the image displayed by an electronic system and the intended or ideal image that the system should display.

Accent. Diacritical mark placed above or below alphabetic characters.

Access time. The time interval between the instant when a computer or control unit calls for a transfer of data to or from a storage device and the instant when this operation is completed. Thus, access time is the sum of the waiting and transfer time. *Note*: In some types of storage, such as disk and drum storage, the access time depends upon the location specified and/or upon preceding events; in other types, such as core storage, the access time is essentially constant.

Accuracy. (1) The degree to which a calculation or measure expressed quantitatively correctly represents its actual value in nature; (2) a statement or measure of the magnitude of error or the range of error inherent to a quantitized value.

Acetate film (acetate base). Safety film whose base essentially consists of cellulose acetate or triacetate.

Acronym. A word formed from the initial letter or letters of the words in a name or phrase; e.g., ALGOL from ALGOrithmic Language, and COBOL from common Business oriented Language.

Acuity (visual). The ability of the eye to distinguish small spatial separations and small objects in a visual field. It varies with contrast, luminance, and the kind of object.

Alignment. (1) Proper positioning of printed characters; (2) proper positioning of the frames recorded on a microfilm or microfiche; (3) proper positioning of prepared forms slide format or prepared stored format upon the data image recorded on microfilm.

Alphanumeric characters. Designating both alphanumeric and numeric characters.

Analog (as opposed to digital). The use of electrical analogies (e.g., varying voltages, frequencies) by which a continuous signal rather than a series of pulses represents quantitative values. Voltages that represent the intended magnitude of electron-beam deflection or the coordinate position of the beam on a CRT screen are examples.

Analog computer. A computer that subjects electric analogies to various constraints as defined by an equation or a system of equations for the purpose of determining numerical data.

Aperture. (1) In an optical system, an opening; (2) in a microreproduction system, the cutaway in a card into which a segment of microfilm is inserted.

Aperture card. A card with one or more rectangular holes or cutaways, each of which holds a frame or frame of microfilm.

Archival quality. The ability of processed photographic material to resist deterioration over a long, specified time period; (2) the extent to which processed film maintains its original characteristics over a specified period of use and storage.

Arithmetic operation. Elementary arithmetic that is performed on numerical quantities in a computer.

Array. A group of items arranged or structured in an ordered pattern.

Example 1: A one-dimensional array (i.e., a list) of one-word items:

Adams
Baker
Collins
Dorsey

Example 2: A two-dimensional array (i.e., a matrix) of one-digit items:

7	2	5	4
3	8	0	9
6	9	1	6
4	7	3	8

Example 3: A single row of light-emitting diodes.

Auxiliary storage. Storage that supplements computer working storage. Synonymous with backup storage, mass storage, and secondary storage. *Note:* In general, auxiliary storage has a much larger capacity but a longer access time than working storage. Usually, the computer cannot access auxiliary storage directly for instructions or instruction operands.

Availability. The period of time, usually quoted by an equipment manufacturer, expected to elapse between placement of a nonpriority order for a particular type of equipment and delivery of the equipment to the user.

Band. (1) A group of tracks (usually in a disk storage or drum storage unit) associated for some specific purpose; e.g., a group of eight tracks that are read and recorded upon in parallel to permit high-speed transfers of 8-bit bytes of data; (2) the range of frequencies between two defined limits.

Bandwidth. The difference, expressed in hertz, between the highest and lowest frequencies of a band.

BCD *(Binary coded decimal).* Pertaining to a method of representing each of the decimal digits 0 through 9 by a distinct group of binary digits. For example, in the "8-4-2-1" BCD notation, which is used in numerous digital computers, the decimal number 39 is represented as 0011 1001 (whereas in pure binary notation it would be represented as 100111).

Binary. Pertaining to the number system with a radix of 2, or to a characteristic or property involving a choice or condition in which there are two possibilities.

Bit. A binary digit; a digit (0 or 1) in the representation of a number in binary notation.

Black line. Polarity of a CRT image should be specified. CRT images produced by standard procedures are regarded as black line and positive.

Blemish. An extraneous microscopic spot on film, usually reddish or yellowish in color.

Blister. (1) A fault in photographic materials whereby emulsion detaches from the film base and forms a bubble; (2) in optics, an elliptical bubble or seed.

Blowback. The enlargement of microimages to readable form.

Boldface. Type characters with thick, dark strokes and curves.

Buffer. A storage device used to compensate for differences in the rates of flow of data or in the times of occurrence of events when transmitting data from one device to another. For example, a buffer holding one line is associated with most line printers to compensate for the large difference between the high speed at which the computer can transmit data to the printer and the relatively low speed of the printing operation itself.

Byte. A group of adjacent bits operated upon as a unit and usually shorter than a word. *Note:* In a number of important current computer systems, the term "byte" has been assigned the more specific meaning of a group of eight adjacent bits, which can represent one alphanumeric character or two decimal digits.

Camera, Step and repeat. A type of camera that can expose separate images on different portions of a film.

Card. Usually the same as punched card, which is characterized by successive columns of numbers into which holes are punched to represent data, symbols, or control information. Other cards that have coded notches along an edge, punched holes denoting symbols close to an edge, or data encoded in magnetic strips are not important to computer output microfilm.

Carriage return. In a character-by-character printing mechanism, this operation causes the next character to be printed at the left margin.

Cathode-ray tube. An electronic vacuum tube containing a screen on which information can be stored or displayed. The abbreviation CRT is frequently used. *Note:* Cathode-ray tubes served as the principal storage medium in some of the early digital computers; they now serve as the basic component of most display units.

Character. A member of a set of mutually distinct marks or signals used to represent data. Each member has one or more conventional representations on paper (e.g., a letter of the ordinary alphabet) and/or in data processing equipment (e.g., a particular configuration of 0 and 1 bits).

Character density. The maximum number of characters that can be stored in a given unit of length; e.g., 200/556/800 bits per inch.

Character generation. The electronic generation of characters on a display surface such as the face of a CRT.

Character generator. A device or circuit network that translates coded signals into visible characters on a suitable display or imprints them on film.

Character reader. A device that translates data from human-readable characters directly into machine-readable characters.

Character set. (1) A set of mutually distinct marks or signals used to represent data; e.g., a typical character set for a printer might include the digits 0 through 9, the letters A through Z, and the common punctuation marks. (2) The set of alphanumerics and symbols inherent to a display, printing, recording, or plotting system.

Character transfer rate. The rate at which characters are transferred from one location to another.

Chip. (1) A tiny piece of semiconductor material containing the equivalent of many cascaded, active electronic circuits. (2) A piece of microfilm containing one or several microimages (often referred to as fiche or microfiche unless the film segment is itself part of a larger unit of some kind, like a microfiche).

Chromatic aberration. A lens defect that precludes true or authentic reconstruction of colors or focusing of all such colors at the same time.

CIM. Computer input microfilm.

Cine orientation. Roll microfilm with the individual frames arranged one under the other as if they were frames on a reel of motion-picture film.

Circuit. (1) A closed system of conductors and related elements through which electric current can flow; (2) a communications link between two or more points.

Clear. (1) To "erase" (i.e., delete) the data in a storage location or device by bringing all storage cells involved to a prescribed state, usually the state denoting zero or blank; (2) similarly, to erase a display from a CRT screen.

Coating. A thin layer applied to a base material, such as film, plastic, or metal.

Code. A set of unambiguous rules that specifies the exact manner by which data is to be represented by the characters of a character set; e.g., ASCII, Hollerith code. A complete set or formulation of unambiguous rules that define character or symbol designations and further specify how they shall represent data or define operations. ASCII, EBCDIC, Hollerith are all distinct codes.

Comic-strip orientation. Roll microfilm with individual frames arranged side by side along the film length, like the frames of a comic strip.

Command. (1) A control signal, especially one transmitted from a computer to a peripheral device or input-output channel; (2) loosely, an instruction.

Compatibility. The characteristic that enables one device to accept and process data prepared by another device without prior code translation, data transcription, or other modifications. Thus, one computer system is "data-compatible" with another if it can read and process the punched cards, magnetic tape, etc., produced by the other computer system. *See also* Program compatibility.

Computer. A device that automatically solves numerical or logical problems by processing incoming data in accordance with a set of rules and procedures, as prescribed by an operational program, and delivers the results of these operations in coded form to a suitable output device(s).

Computer graphics. Pictorial or diagrammatic structures synthesized by a computer and displayed on an image-forming device such as a CRT, or recorded on film, or some other medium.

Configuration. A specific set of equipment units interconnected and (in the case of a computer) programmed to operate as a system. Thus, a computer configuration consists of one or more central processors, one or more storage devices, and one or more input-output devices. Synonymous with system configuration.

Contact print. A photographic print exposed with its emulsion in contact with the negative or positive transparency being copied.

Contrast. The difference in brightness between two parts of a visual field.

Control card. A punched card that contains input data required for a specific application of a general routine such as a generator or operating system; e.g., one of a series of cards that direct an operating system to load and initiate execution of a particular program.

Control panel. (1) A part of a computer console that contains manual controls such as switches, buttons, and dials; (2) same as plugboard.

Crosstalk. Undesirable signals in a channel, initiated by another channel in the same system.

CRT. See Cathode-ray tube.

Darkroom. A lighttight room used for loading and unloading and developing exposed photographic film or paper.

Data. Any representation of a fact or idea in a form capable of being communicated or manipulated by some process. The representation may be more suitable for interpretation by either humans (e.g., printed text) or equipment (e.g., punched cards or electric signals). *Note:* Information, a closely related term, is the meaning that humans assign to data by means of the known conventions used in its representation.

Data storage and retrieval systems. Data storage and retrieval systems have as their main function the storage of file items for later reuse rather than modification, and most often to maintain the file items unaltered, with the exception of updating and purging.

Definition. The resolution and sharpness of an image.

Developer. A chemical reagent used to produce visible image on an exposed photographic layer. It may take many forms for different materials, such as conventional formulas for silver emulsions, plain water used to develop blueprints, or a gas (such as ammonia vapor used to develop diazo films and prints).

Diagram. A representation of a sequence of operations or the arrangement of circuits within a device. A diagram is less symbolic than a flow chart.

Diazo material. A slow print film or paper employing diazonium salts that form an image after exposure to light strong in the blue-to-ultraviolet spectrum.

Diazo process. A copying process utilizing a film or paper that has been sensitized by diazonium salts. Upon exposure to blue or ultraviolet light, it forms a latent image that can be developed.

Digit. A single numeric character used to represent an integer; e.g., in binary notation, the character 0 or 1; in decimal notation, one of the characters from 0 through 9.

Digital. Pertaining to data represented in the form of digits. *See* analog.

Digital computer. A computer that operates on digital data by performing arithmetic and logical operations on the data. Contrast with *analog computer.*

Direct access. See Random access.

Direct image film. Film that produces a negative from a negative and a positive from a positive without reversal processing.

Direct positive. A positive image obtained directly from another positive image without the use of a negative intermediate. This process will also produce a negative from a negative directly.

Display. Any mechanism for presenting information to the user via one or more of the senses.

Document. (1) A medium and the data recorded on it for human use (e.g., a check, report sheet, or book); (2) by extension, any record that has permanence and can be read by man and/or machine.

Dot matrix. A matrix of dots that forms any specified character of a character set when appropriate individual elements are activated to emit light.

Downtime. The period of time during which a computer or other equipment is unavailable for productive use because of a mechanical or electronic fault or malfunction. Downtime includes time wasted on runs spoiled by faults, time lost while awaiting repairs, and the repair time itself. *See* Uptime.

Duo process. A microfilming process using a flow camera that records two dissimilar rows of unevenly aligned microimages, each row utilizing half the width of the film. Often the camera records down a row in one direction and up a second row in the opposite direction.

Duplex process. A method using flow microfilm cameras whereby front and back of documents are simultaneously photographed side by side onto the film; COM recorders also achieve this effect.

EBR. Electron beam recorder.

Edit. To modify the form or format of data. Editing may involve the rearrangement of data, the addition of data (e.g., insertion of dollar signs and decimal points), the deletion of data (e.g., suppression of leading zeros), code translation, and the control of layouts for printing (e.g., provision of headings and page numbers).

EDP. Electronic data processing.

Emulsion. A suspension of light-sensitive materials (e.g., silver halides) suitable for use as a photographic coating.

Enlarger. A device for making a large photographic print of a smaller original.

Film, Direct positive. Film that reproduces positive originals as positives and negative originals as negatives.

Film frame. The area exposed to light through the camera optical system during one exposure.

Film, Negative. Film on which images of dark objects will appear light and images of light objects will appear dark.

Film, Nonperforated. Roll film without sprocket holes.

Film, Panchromatic. A black-and-white film sensitive to the entire visible spectrum.

Film, Perforated. Roll film with sprocket holes.

Film, Positive. Film on which images of dark objects appear dark and images of light objects appear light.

Film, Reversal. A film processed to produce a positive image instead of the customary negative one.

Film, Roll. Film wound on a core, reel, or spool.

Film, Sheet. Film precut into rectangular form.

Film strip. A short strip of processed film containing a number of frames.

Fixer. A solution used to remove undeveloped particles from the emulsion, thus preventing further development.

Flats. Two pieces of very smooth and level glass, highly polished; used for holding film in readers and enlargers.

Flip-flop. A device that has two interchangeable states; e.g., a toggle switch.

Flying spot. A small rapidly moving spot of light, usually generated by a CRT, used to illuminate successive spots of a surface containing dark and light areas. A phototube detects the amount of light reflected and produces electronic signals that define the surface.

Format. The arrangement and positioning of information within a display.

Font. A set of characters allied with respect to size and style.

Forms flash (forms overlay). The process of precisely superimposing predetermined document formats on a frame of computer output data. Two methods are currently in use: (1) optical flash or strobing technique whereby a film or glass-slide image is projected onto the specified microfilm area and (2) software generation of the format, which is appropriately merged with the data.

Grain size. The size of the particles of silver halide in an emulsion. The inherent grain size of microfilm is very fine. Exposure and processing affect grain size.

Halide. A binary chemical compound of a halogen (chlorine, iodine, bromine, fluorine) with a more electropositive element or group. The light-sensitive materials in silver emulsions are silver bromide, silver chloride, and silver iodide.

Hard copy. A printed copy of machine output in readable form for human beings; for example, reports, listings, documents, summaries.

Hardware. Physical equipment such as mechanical, magnetic, electrical, and electronic devices. *See* Software.

Hypo. Ammonium or sodium thiosulfate; agents used to remove unexposed silver halides from silver emulsion film. The term commonly refers to a fixer solution, which may also contain certain acids or hardening agents.

Hypo, Residual. The amount of fixer solution remaining in film or paper after it has been washed.

Image, Latent. The invisible image produced by radiant energy falling on a photosensitive surface. The process of development makes the image visible.

Image area. The part of the frame or recording area on film intended for the image (data or graphic forms).

Information retrieval. That branch of computer technology concerned with techniques for storing and searching large quantities of information and making selected information available. An information retrieval system may or may not be a real-time system.

Infrared. Pertaining to, or being, electromagnetic radiation having wavelengths greater than those of visible light (beyond the red end of the spectrum) and shorter than those of microwaves.

Input. The data to be processed.

Integrated circuit. A complete, complex electronic circuit, capable of performing all the functions of a conventional circuit containing numerous discrete transistors, diodes, capacitors, and/or resistors, all of whose component parts are fabricated and assembled in a single integrated process.

Interblock gap. The distance between the end of one block and the beginning of the next block on a magnetic tape. The tape can be stopped and brought up to normal speed again in this distance, and no reading or writing is permitted in the interblock gap because the tape speed may be changing. Synonymous with inter-record gap and record gap (but use of these two terms is not recommended because of the important distinction between blocks and records).

Interface. A shared boundary; for example, the boundary between two subsystems or two devices.

Italics. Slanted characters.

Jackets. Transparent envelopes used to simulate microfiche formatting.

Keystoning. Distortion that occurs when the lens used in photographing the CRT is off axis and the image so formed is larger on one side than the other.

Kilocycle. A thousand cycles.

LED. Light-emitting diode.

Lightface. Normal character intensity as opposed to boldface.

Light-emitting diode. Diodes made of semiconductor materials that have the ability to radiate light, usually in the red or infrared portions of the spectrum, when electric current passes through the diode.

Light-sensitive materials. Substances that undergo changes upon exposure to light. The most common light-sensitive photographic materials in films and papers are silver halides, diazo dyes, diazonium salts, bichromated gelatin, and the photoconductive materials employed in xerography.

Lower case. The small letters of a type font.

Magnetic drum. A storage device; data is recorded on a cylinder having a surface coating of magnetic material.

MICR. Magnetic-ink character recognition. Machine recognition of characters printed with magnetic ink. *See* OCR.

Microfiche. A sheet of microfilm comprising multiple uniform-sized microimages arranged in a grid pattern. It usually has a title that can be read without a magnifier.

Microfont. An upper case font designed by the *NMA* for microfilm applications.

Microform. Any arrangement of images reduced in size; or any form, either film or paper, that contains microimages.

Micrographics. The creation, recording, imprinting, or drawing of images, including alphanumerics, on a microformat.

Microimage. Any unit of information, such as a drawing or a page of text, that is too small to be read without a magnifier.

Micromation. A particular form of micrographics comprising any systemized process of automatically transferring computer-generated data to a microformat. The outstanding example of micromation is computer output microfilming (COM). A marginal qualifier might be printer output microfilming (POM), a procedure for transferring computer output printed on standard paper forms to a microformat.

Micropublishing. Issuing books in microfilm form.

Microwave. All electromagnetic waves in the radio-frequency spectrum above 890 megacycles per second.

Negative or negative appearing image. A photographic image in which the light areas of the object represented appear dark and the dark areas appear light.

Network. (1) A series of points interconnected by communications channels. (2) The switched telephone network is the network of telephone lines normally used for dialed telephone calls. (3) A private line network is a network of communications channels confined to the use of one customer.

Notation. A system of representing items by a set of marks, signs, figures, or characters.

OCR. Optical character recognition. The machine recognition of printed or written characters based on inputs from photoelectric transducers. *See* MICR.

OEM. Original equipment manufacture, i.e., equipment manufactured for use as a component in a system manufactured by another company.

Off-line. Pertaining to equipment or devices not under direct control of the central processing unit. May also be used to describe terminal equipment not connected to a transmission line.

Optical system. A system comprising all parts of a photographic lens and accessory elements that contribute to the formation of an image on a photographic film or on a viewing screen.

Output. Data that has been processed.

Paper-tape reader. A device that senses data punched as a series of holes in paper tape.

Perforator. A keyboard device for punching paper tape.

Permanent storage. A method or device for retaining the results of processing outside the machine; usually punched cards or magnetic tape.

Pinboard. A perforated composition board in which connections are made by manually inserted pins for the purpose of setting some part of the internal operation of a computer or to effect some desired operation in some other kind of data processing equipment, e.g., a COM recorder.

Plugboard. A perforated board used to control the operation of some automatic data processing equipment. The holes in the board (called "hubs" or "sockets") are manually interconnected in a manner appropriate to the job to be performed by means of wires terminating in plugs (called "patchcords"). Synonymous with control panel. *See also* Pinboard.

Polarity. The tonal relationship of an image, with respect to the original, that is either positive or negative.

POM. Printer output microfilming. *See also* Micromation.

Positive or positive appearing image. A photographic image with dark lines, characters, and neutral tones on a light background.

Positive film. Film having the same polarity as the original image or film.

Printer output microfilming (POM.). A systemized procedure for automatically photographing standard computer printout sheets generated by impact printers and transferring the images to microfilm according to a predetermined format, usually a microfiche.

Print-out. See Hard copy.

Processing. The treating of exposed photographic material to make the latent image visible. It consists of developing, fixing, washing, and drying the exposed material.

Processor (film). A device for carrying out film processing.

Program compatibility. A characteristic of programs, computers, or both whereby a program written for one computer system can be executed by another to produce identical results. Computer output microfilm is generally impeded by lack of program compatibility, i.e., format instructions on tape intended for a particular COM recorder will not properly operate another recorder, and software developed for a particular recorder cannot be used by another. Sometimes, however, special software can be developed for a COM equipped with an internal processor so that the codes of other software are automatically translated into language employed by that recorder.

Pull-down. The distance that film is moved after exposure.

Random access. Pertaining to a storage device for which the time required to access or recapture a designated item is never more than a specified maximum or significantly less regardless of its storage location.

Real time. (1) Pertaining to the actual time during which a physical process takes place. (2) Pertaining to the performance of a computation during a period short in comparison with the actual time that the related physical process takes place in order that results of the computations can be used in guiding the physical process.

Reduction. The number of times or scale by which a given linear dimension of an object is reduced when it is photographed.

Reduction Ratio. The ratio of reduction units to one (20:1 reduction ratio is equivalent to 20X).

Repeatability. The accuracy with which a system may be made to record successively in the same geometric location within a frame.

Resolvable horizontal lines. The maximum number of visually distinguishable horizontal lines which can be recorded within a specified image.

Resolvable line pitch. The ratio of the number of resolvable lines to the image dimension (in mm) perpendicular to the resolvable lines, and equal to lines per mm.

Resolvable vertical lines. The maximum number of visually distinguishable vertical lines which can be recorded within a specified image.

Retrieval coding. Indexing methods for manual or automatic retrieval of images.

Reversal processing. A microfilm processing technique by which the polarity of the microfilm image is reversed as compared with conventional processing. *See also* Direct-image film; Polarity.

Roman. The nonitalic, regular vertical form of a character.

Rotated image. See Cine orientation.

Sans serif. Characters without serifs.

Screen. The surface of an electrostatic cathode-ray storage tube on which electrostatic charges are stored and information is thus temporarily displayed.

Semiconductor. A solid whose electrical conductivity lies between the high conductivities of metals and the low conductivities of insulators. *Note:* Transistors and crystal diodes are semiconductor circuit elements used in many computers and COM recorders.

Serif. The short line, cross-bar or embellishment extending from or at an angle to the upper and lower ends of a character.

Silver film. Film utilizing light-sensitive silver halide salts that are normally processed by wet solutions.

Software. The collection of programs and routines associated with a computer (such as assemblers, compilers, utility routines, and operating systems) which facilitate the programming and operation of the computer. *See also* Hardware.

Storage register. A register in a storage unit of a computer.

Stroke. A straight line or arc used as a segment of a graphic character.

Stroke generation. A method of generating characters that joins short strokes in a manner similar to that used in ordinary handwriting.

Texture characters. Graphic characters having a standard shape that may be joined together to produce bar charts or plots.

Throughput. The total amount of useful work performed by a data processing or a COM recorder system during a given period of time.

Upper case. Capital letters.

Uptime. The period of time during which a computer or other equipment is available for productive use; that is when it has the power turned on, is not undergoing maintenance work, and is known or believed to be operating correctly. Synonymous with available time. *See also* Downtime.

Vector generator. A method of generating graphical information using direction and line length.

Vesicular film. Film in which the light-sensitive element is suspended in a plastic layer, and which upon exposure forms a latent image by creating strains within the layer. Heating the plastic layer releases the strains and makes the latent image visual. When the layer cools, the image becomes permanent.

White line. Dark film with information carried as white clear lines. Reverse processed COM film is white line.

INDEX